Home

Can Be a

Happy Place

by Knofel Staton

A Division of Standard Publishing
Cincinnati, Ohio
40-008

Library of Congress Catalog Card No 74-84669
ISBN: 0-87239-009-8

© 1975
The STANDARD PUBLISHING Company
Cincinnati, Ohio
Printed in U.S.A.

Introduction

The need of meaningful sharing (giving and taking) within the community is felt by every human. No one should live alone; indeed, no one develops well alone. God has made it clear that human development comes through interpersonal sharing in love. Yet the development of "man made in God's image" is facing a powerful enemy called individualism, which threatens to destroy the concept of the community. One of the tragedies of this battle is that whatever threatens the individual's community also threatens the community's individual. Nowhere is this more vividly seen than in the smallest community, the home.

The separate schedules of family members keep people apart. The television set tends to make us more cloistered than communicative. The automobile pulls us away from home. Rather than heightening our individual maturity by each person "doing his own thing," unmet needs of the individuals emerge. Some persons run away from home to live in a commune where interpersonal sharing can take place. Some experiment with the drug and the occult culture, trying to discover or extend their selfhood through a kind of "mental community." Small sharing groups are becoming a popular experience for many.

Since the truth that people need people is becoming once more evident, it is not surprising to find a renewed interest in the family. Contemporary literature reflects a high interest in the family, even though contemporary life reveals a limited involvement in satisfying family living. The rise in the divorce rate, along with the high sale of books about family living, indicates an interest in how to succeed in family life. One tragedy is that many who are not divorced do not feel they have succeeded. They are married, but not happy.

Is there any infallible guide to successful family living? That depends on how we measure "success." If success is measured by our own wishes, the answer is no. The success of anything cannot have desire as the criterion for evaluation. The success of anything is measured by whether or not it is functioning according to its design. I might wish that my car could fly, but I can't say it is a flop if it doesn't. I must consider the car's designed purpose, and I must also determine whether or not I have treated it according to that design. It is the same when evaluating success within a family.

We must begin our search for successful family life by consulting our God-ufactured guide, the Bible. In this guide we find both the purpose for the family and the designed roles of individuals within the family. Through living Bible-based principles, a happy family will result. No shortcut will work. Gimmicks must give way to God. Strategies of men must give way to the Spirit of God. Selfishness must give way to sacrifice. Only then will we be on the road to becoming the kind of people God intended, people created in His image and living lives worth sharing and developing, lives that foster "common oneness" in the home.

Let us consider God's design for the family. But let us do it with the willingness to change whatever needs changing. Being happy in the home depends greatly upon what kind of person each member is becoming, for this affects what kind of persons the other family members can become.

—*Knofel Staton*

Every Scripture quotation identified NASB is from *The New American Standard Bible and New Testament*. By permission of The Lockman Foundation, F. D. Lockman, President.

Contents

1

The First Family

The union of the first human family was not an afterthought of God, but was the crown of His creation. He knew that His creation was good—the light, the atmosphere, land, seas, vegetation, celestial bodies, and animal life (Genesis 1:4-25). Then God made the male human being, and for the first time God said that something was not good about His creation: "It is not good that the man should be alone" (2:18). Why? What was not good about it?

Only a superficial reading of the Bible makes us see that our fellowship with God is not complete apart from our fellowship with others. That is why Jesus made it clear that love for both God and others is the core of the law and prophets (Matthew 22:37-40). He came in person to demonstrate it. One's love is incomplete unless it includes both God and others (1 John 4:20). This is because God's love dwells in the Christian (John 15:9; Romans 5:5; Galatians 5:22). God loves people, and we also are to love people (1 John 4:12). Because of his need to express love to another person, Adam's love would have not been complete without another person. Because he had special needs as a male, his life would not have been complete without a woman. This fact was clear to Adam after he had reviewed all other life that had been formed from the earth (Genesis 2:20). Humanity must note this truth. Some individuals have been tempted to try to fill up the empty space of life with pets, but pets will not meet our basic need for a corresponding partner.

God knew that the male (and society) needed the balance of womanhood: "I will make him a helper fit for him." These words reveal a significant truth; the woman is God's special provision for the man. The Hebrew word for "helper" is normally used elsewhere in the Old Testament to refer to God's help (Exodus 18:4; Deuteronomy 33:7, 26, 29; Psalms 20:2; 33:20; 89:19; 115:9-11; 121:1, 2; 124:8; 146:5). Except for the usage in Genesis 2, it is used in a negative way when referring to human help (Isaiah 30:5; Ezekiel 12:14; Daniel 11:34; Hosea 13:9).

Why would a word, normally used to refer to God's aid, be used to refer to the woman's aid? The answer seems clear: God helps the male through the woman. She is God's assistant in meeting man's needs; indeed, she is a special ambassador of God. It is little wonder that after God created the woman, for the first time He saw that His creation was *very* good (Genesis 1:31). The woman fills in where the man is lacking.

God certainly did not create the man to live independently of the woman. Male chauvinism will not square with the Master's creation. God created each sex with the other in mind. Sex differences are God's design for balanced humanity. Male and female are different in more than just their physical design. Sex refers to the whole person, not just the physique. Woman's physique is designed to house and nourish new life, and her total personality matches that characteristic. The male's physique is designed to be aggressive, and his personality matches that characteristic. While the male is more concerned with the conquering and mastering, the woman brings the needed balance of peacemaking and tenderness.

The differences between male and female are seen at many other levels. The male usually handles large tasks well but tends to be impatient and clumsy with small things, while the woman handles small details well. The male tends to be more direct and business-like in his relationships, while the woman tends to be more personal in hers. The male thinks things through

8

more objectively, while the woman feels them through.

After Adam was convinced of his incompleteness, God made the woman out of the man (Genesis 2:21, 22; 1 Corinthians 11:8, 9). That she was made from man's rib reveals two things:

First, the woman was initially made of man-material. God "built" (Hebrew word for "made" in Genesis 2:22) the female from man. She was not just a part of him, but had a part of him. Every woman has a part of man's nature, and from the first conception every man has a part of woman's nature. Thus neither is complete until he or she gets the other part back in the union of marriage. Neither is independent of the other (1 Corinthians 7:4; 11:11, 12). Only as each person is complemented by the other can he reach his potential as a human; the only exception is if a person has a special gift of celibacy (1 Corinthians 7:7).

Adam immediately recognized his counterpart as his partner, not as his property. He declared, "This is now [Where have you been all my life?] bone of my bones, and flesh of my flesh [You are my counterpart! I've found you! Whoopee!]." She was called woman (a female-man), because she was taken out of man. Male pride has a difficult time with this truth. To suggest that the woman is an inferior creature is to degrade the first product God produced out of man. Let man never forget that the woman was fashioned out of his own stuff by the Master Designer himself.

Second, woman's special design with man's needs in mind provides the foundation for the fellowship, communication, sharing, and the unity of the male and the female. This is made clear in Genesis 2:24, 25: "Therefore [for this reason, that woman is made from man] shall a man leave his father and his mother, and shall cleave unto his wife: and they shall be one flesh. And they were both naked, the man and his wife, and were not ashamed." We cannot find the slightest suggestion that either male or female was created inferior or superior to the other. Rather, we find that by complementing one another, together they bring about the needed balance of God's characteristics. God's image is not bottled up in either male or female alone, but in both. In God's own personhood, He maintains the balance of conquering (male characteristic) and caring (female characteristic), of protecting (female characteristic) and penetrating (male characteristic). It is through the balance of the first male and female that God's image is beamed to our world (Genesis 1:27, 28; 5:1, 2). The word "man" in Genesis 1:27 refers to humanity, the combination of male and female created on the sixth day. Genesis 5:1, 2, clarifies this: "When God created man [humanity], He made him [corporate pronoun for humanity] in the likeness of God. He created them male and female, and He blessed them and named them [male and female] Man [humanity] in the day when they were created"; NASB.

The first male and female formed a family unit (Genesis 2:24). God blessed Adam and Eve and shared with them something of His own kind of responsibilities. For instance, God was involved in a creating function, and He shared this with the two: "Multiply, and fill the earth" (1:28; NASB). As neither male nor female can do this alone, neither can one of them fulfill the rest of God's shared functions alone. God shared His dominating function with the unit (1:28). He also shared His caring function (2:15). The balance between dominating and caring required both the male and female working together. Perversion began when one acted independently of the other (Genesis 3).

God did not rest from His initial creative activity nor consider that it was *very good* until the formation of this first family. Human activity began in a family union (2:24 ff.) and will be consummated in a family union (Revelation 21:2). Between Genesis and Revelation the family is one key model for meaningful relationships between God and man and between man and fellowman. When man became estranged from God, He considered the united family as a goal for His people. Thus His reconciled people are called "members" in His household (Ephesians 4:25; 2:19). They are called His children in 1 John 2, and brothers and sisters of each other in Matthew 12:50 and James 2:15. Reconciliation with Christ is likened to a marriage, the church the bride and Jesus the bridegroom (Revelation 21:2, 9; John 3:29). It is interesting to note that in the New Testament the members of the church are called "saints," a word used in secular Greek to refer to the wife a man had selected for himself. As a wife belongs to her husband, so a Christian belongs to Christ (Ephesians 5:21-33).

Within God's family there is a diversity of personalities and abilities, but this diversity is God's way of meeting the needs of people (1 Corinthians 12:12-28). It is the same with the family. Differences will abound, but harmony depends upon our commitment to God's foundational stones for a marriage. We shall now consider God's foundation for a happy family.

2

God's Recipe for Marriage

God's recipe for successful and permanent marriage has three basic ingredients, and these are found in Genesis 2:24. Each of these ingredients can be likened to a leg of a three-legged stool. If any leg is defective, the stool is unstable and wobbly. This does not mean that the stool no longer exists, but the weak leg needs special attention in order to restore its stability. So it is with the family. Both husband and wife need all three ingredients if their marriage is to be one that will meet the needs of each person. Children need the security of these ingredients in the lives of the mother and father. What are these three "legs" that support a marriage?

Leaving

"Therefore, a man leaves his father and his mother—" A responsible man takes the initiative to leave, and mature parents allow him to do so. This leg is weakened when either the son will not cut the apron strings, or one or both of the parents will not allow the strings to be cut. In some cases, the blame may fall on both the son and the parents.

Leaving is necessary, for without it the son will not have the freedom to function as the head of his new family unit. Without that leaving he cannot cleave to his wife properly. A man cannot cleave to both his wife and his parents.

What is meant by "leaving"? First let us consider what is not meant. It does not mean the abandonment of respect for parents. The commandment to honor father and mother is not canceled with the new marriage. Neither does it mean deserting or not caring for parents. In fact, the command to honor father and mother refers not only to obedience while one is maturing, but also to a responsibility to meet the needs of the parents. This is true especially when the parents are old and dependent. The following Scriptures support this view: Deuteronomy 21:18 ff.; Matthew 15:1-9; Mark 7:1-13; 1 Timothy 5:4. Jesus clearly connected the providing of care for parents with the command to honor father and mother. His teachings on this point have received little attention in our efforts to restore New Testament Christianity. Jesus condemned a stewardship that supported religious programs while neglecting the needs of parents. He said such action "made void the word of God" (Matthew 15:6; Mark 7:13). He was so strong on this point that He connected the prophecy of Isaiah 29:13 to this practice: "This people draweth nigh unto me with their mouth, and honoureth me with their lips; but their heart is far from me. But in vain they do worship me, teaching for doctrines the commandments of men" (Matthew 15:8).

What about the use of public welfare for the care of parents? Each person will have to make his own decision on this issue, but it does seem that such a program was God's intention for His people. In New Testament times there was a state program to care for the poor, but Paul does not include it as a source for parental care. Instead, he calls upon the parents to care for themselves if they are able. If not, they are the children's responsibility. If there are no children, these folk are the church's responsibility. The early church took this responsibility seriously (1 Timothy 5; Acts 6:1-3). The twentieth-century church is just as capable of accepting this responsibility.

While leaving father and mother does not mean abandoning responsible care for them, it does mean no longer depending upon them to meet the basic human needs. After marriage these basic human needs are

13

met by the mate who is the suitable helper. In this new relationship, one can continue to progress into maturity rather than regress into childhood. This maturing process depends partly upon one's ability to look elsewhere than to the parents for supportive security or to fill up the empty places in his life.

Leaving also calls for parental understanding in upbringing. Children must be prepared for this, if they are to have a happy marriage and a balanced family life. If one partner in a marriage does not cleave to the other (because he has not left his parents), that partner may begin to cleave to the children or some other substitute. The person may need the children's dependency so badly he may never let them leave. Cleaving to children rather than to one's mate causes an unhealthy family relationship to develop. Such a person does not mature as he should. If you are not ready to leave your father and mother and invest your life in another's, you are not ready for marriage.

Cleaving

Leaving permits cleaving. A man is to experience not only a leaving, but also a new cleaving relationship. Cleaving to one's wife is as important to the man's continuing self-development, and thus to what he is able to contribute to the new relationship, as is leaving father and mother. If a man does not cleave to his wife, a vacuum will develop in his life. The same is true of the wife. If the husband and wife do not cleave to one another, they will each adopt a substitute. The substitute may be a job, a friend, a personal project, children, or material things. Any substitute that comes between the cleaving of husband and wife whittles down the second leg.

What is meant by the words "to cleave"? What responsibilities accompany the cleaving relationship? The Hebrew word for "cleave" basically means a joining, but the implications are much stronger. It is used to mean the opposite of withdrawing from a person (2 Kings 18:6). It means a determined and devoted persistence to stay with a person (Ruth 1:14). It describes a stick-to-itiveness, a gluing or cementing together (Deuteronomy 13:17; Ezekiel 29:4; Job 19:20; Psalms 22:15; 119:31; Jeremiah 13:11; Lamentations 4:4). The husband and wife should be closer to each other than to any other persons. Nothing should come between the two, for when they are "glued together" they function as one.

The coming of children into the family is no exception. It is wrong for a wife or husband to begin to cling to children more than to the married partner. When this happens, a leg of the marriage is weakened. Besides, the children are hurt rather than helped. The best thing a mother can do for her children is to stick to the father with love, and the best thing a father can do for his children is to stick to the mother with love. The children will have difficulty in respecting the parents if they do not have mutual love and respect for each other.

Parent-child responsibilities are temporary, while the husband-wife responsibilities are permanent. The husband and wife should therefore build their lives around each other with Christ in the center. When all the children are grown and leave home, the husband and wife are left with each other. This is a difficult adjustment, if their lives have not been built around each other. If the children are allowed to weaken the cement of the marriage, the marriage may fall apart when the children are gone.

The words "to cleave to" also emphasize the physical union of the two persons. The Greek translation of the Hebrew word is often used for the intimate association of sexual intercourse. This is the sharing of one total person with another total person. This is such a blending of the two mates that each is united with the other. It is an act of companionship, communication,

commitment, completion, and a "common oneness."
A marriage needs the sexual expression; the prohibi-
tion of it invites problems (1 Corinthians 7:3-5).

Cleaving to a person also connotes a unity of purpose and goals. Thus there are responsibilities that
naturally accompany the relationship, and the couple
must be as devoted to these responsibilities as they are
to each other. We get a clear picture of these responsibilities when we examine those Scripture passages
that describe our cleaving relationship with God. To
cleave to God involves being people of praise
(Jeremiah 13:11). The man who cleaves to his wife will
praise her (Proverbs 31:28). To cleave to God involves
rejecting other gods and their ways (Joshua 23:8). To
cleave to wife is to reject other women. Cleaving to
God is loving Him (Deuteronomy 11:22; 30:20; Joshua
22:5), respecting and serving Him (Deuteronomy
10:20; 13:4; "fear" means respect), and walking in His
ways (Deuteronomy 5:33; Psalm 119: 2, 3). Likewise a
man and wife must love one another, respect one
another, submit to one another, and walk together in
fulfilling their common goal and purpose.

Cleaving, therefore, forms a community, a common
oneness. It is another way to describe the New Testament term "fellowship" (*koinonia*, "common
mind"). The Greek word equivalent to the Hebrew
word "cleave" can be used in the New Testament to
describe one who adopts the objectives of another
(Luke 15:15) and one who adopts the way of Christ
(Acts 17:34). It is not by accident that God describes
the relationship of Christ and the church in terms of a
marriage and calls the relationship "common oneness." As Christ cleaves to the church, the husband
and wife should cleave to each other.

One Flesh

What is the meaning of a man and woman becoming
one flesh? It does not mean that the two individuals

are no longer two. It does mean that they share such a common purpose in life that the two become a working and cooperating unit. They do not compete against one another with different goals in mind, but complement one another with a mutual goal. To be "glued together" is to function together.

The same kind of unity is meant when we read that God is one (Deuteronomy 6:4), although He is three: Father, Son, and Holy Spirit. The three form a unit, as Jesus described in John 17. This oneness of purpose allowed Jesus to submit to the Father's will (Matthew 26:42), do the works of the Father (John 5:19, 20), and allowed the Father to honor the Son (Matthew 17:5). The three agreed (1 John 5:7, 8; John 15:26). Jesus said He and the Father were one (John 10:30), and anyone who had seen Him had seen the Father (John 14:9).

The unity of the husband and wife cannot be reduced to a mere physical union. It is broadened to include an emotional, volitional, and spiritual unity, revolving around their goal orientation. Their oneness of spiritual purpose fosters trust between them (Proverbs 31:11). The unit should be so tight that each person acts in the absence of the other the same way he would if the other were present.

I am away from home much of the time, but I know that my wife will make the kind of decisions I would have made were I present. Our goals are the same. I trust her because of our mutuality. Our commonness of goals is not the result of our designing them autonomously, but we worked them out together. Our goals are higher than either of us individually or both of us collectively. We have both adopted God's goals for ourselves and our children, as revealed in His Word. Our goals do not change with the shifting sand. Our unit is stable because the goals around which the unit exists are stable. That means we will not walk one way today and another way tomorrow. We do not have to second-guess what will satisfy the other, or "play games" with each other. Neither do we run back to mother and father for comfort or security.

The sequence of leaving, cleaving, and becoming one flesh is important for a stable marriage, but the most important factor is the purpose each partner has for life. If the goal is stable, the leaving will be settled, the cleaving will be secure, and the unity will be sweet. Too many marriages have broken up because of the lack of a harmonious purpose for living, which opens up the possibility of cleaving to a substitute. Jesus understood that cleaving and oneness formed a working unit (Matthew 19:5; Mark 10:9). His words, "joined together," in these verses come from one Greek word that described a team of oxen yoked together. They work together for a common cause. They depend on one another, and they pull together in the same direction toward that goal. In the same way, marriage is a yoking of two people. To be yoked with a person who has a different goal in life is to be mismated (2 Corinthians 6:14).

A mutual goal enhances openness between two persons. The fact that the first man and woman were naked and not ashamed may be attributed to their openness at every level of life. Hiding from one another (whether it be the body, thoughts, or deeds) is partly due to a lack of common oneness. A shift of goals in the unit causes weakness and problems, hampering the development of each partner. Agreement, cooperation, and trust give way to disagreement, competition, and doubt.

A secure marriage rests upon the interrelationship of leaving, cleaving, and a united life. These foundations (legs) need not wobble or cause the marriage to fall. They can and should be continually strengthened by the application of the Word of God. God must be in the center of our homes. A Christian home is not necessarily where Christians reside, but where Christ rules.

3

The Decision to Marry

Should I Marry?

Two extreme philosophies concerning marriage have been communicated through Christian history. One extreme holds that the single life (celibacy) is a mark of super spirituality. Elevating the single life happened early in Christian history. In fact, as early as the second century, some churches denied membership to married couples. In some instances, baptism was denied unless a person was a virgin, widow, or celibate. A married person, however, could purchase a title to baptism by getting a divorce.

Such overemphasis upon the celibate life fails to note that marriage is the usual state in the Bible, while the single life is the exception. Paul indicated that some of the apostles were married and traveled with their wives (1 Corinthians 9:5). The New Testament writers assumed that marriage and family living were accepted within the life of the church (1 Corinthians 11; Ephesians 5:21-29; Colossians 3:18-21; 1 Peter 3:1) and in the lives of the church leaders (1 Timothy 3:1 ff; Titus 1:6). Jesus challenged divorce as a route to becoming single (Matthew 19; Luke 16:18). Paul made it clear that a Christian should not divorce his mate (Romans 7; 1 Corinthians 7).

Some people use 1 Corinthians 7 to support the spirituality of celibacy; however, every teaching about celibacy in that chapter is balanced by a "but." In this chapter Paul relates his teaching about single life and married life to a person's charisma, or gift, and also to the contemporary world situation (vv. 26, 28). Each person has his own special gift from God (v. 7). Thus neither the single life nor the married life is more

19

spiritual than the other. Either the desire to marry or to remain single can be a result of charisma or of self-ishness. Each person should lead the life to which the Lord has assigned him (v. 17). There is no reason whatever to attach superiority or inferiority to a person's marital status.

Paul's concern for the unmarried to remain single (v. 25) rests upon the situation at that time. He refers to some kind of external distress that would present added difficulty to those in the married state (v. 28). Possibly, Paul is referring to some kind of persecution or hardship. The added trouble could have been that the married person would have to bear the sufferings of his mate as well as his own. It is also possible that Paul refers to the distress caused by the divisions within the Corinthian church, in which family members were no doubt pitted against each other. In the midst of such distress, the married person certainly would be concerned about and share in the troubles of his mate (vv. 32-37). Paul is not condemning marriage because of this; he is simply stating a fact. To Timothy Paul wrote that if anyone does not provide for his family, he is worse than an unbeliever (1 Timothy 5:8). He had made it clear to the Corinthians that a husband should give to his wife her conjugal rights (1 Corinthians 7:3). God's design for marriage is that each mate be a helper for the other (Genesis 2:18). The husband is to love the wife as himself (Ephesians 5:25-30). Thus Paul did not overlook the care that married partners should have for one another (1 Corinthians 7:32-35), or advise against marriage (v. 36).

True, married people are not as free as the single person, to give undivided attention to God's service. This does not make being married a sin; a married person partly fulfills his commitment to God by loving his mate and his family. It would be a sin if the married person's attention were not divided, although it is not a divided attention so much as it is a two-pronged attention. If one neglects either family or God, it is a sin.

On the other extreme, some have placed an over-emphasis on the married state. We live in a society where young adults are often stigmatized as odd if they are not married, or at least living with someone. This is especially true of single women, as seen in our label, "old maids," over against the term "bachelor" for the men. Unmarried adults may be the most uncomfort-able group of people in our churches, not because of their state, but because of other people's reaction to them. They are easily left out of meaningful fellow-ship. We put them in a class called "Pairs and Spares," in which they are the spares during the class period and at the socials. Who wants to be seen as a spare?

In effect we are saying that we are uncomfortable with the unmarried person's single status when we continually try to match him or her, or keep asking, "Don't you ever want to get married?" Why do we often demand that our ministers be married? Some persons think that if a man is married, he will be better able to minister to families and counsel married cou-ples with more insight. That is not necessarily so. Some of our best, most incisive, and most mature ministers are single. God has some fantastic pos-sibilities for single people. We should not hinder their fulfilling them, nor should we consider that the present state of a person must be his future state. The choice or charisma to remain single may be replaced with a need to marry. A married person may lose his mate. Let us be Christian brothers and sisters to each other, encouraging one another in his present status.

Whom Should I Marry?

The first criterion in one's considering marrying a person is that person's spiritual status. The Bible warns against the yoking together of two persons who have different spiritual values and goals. Any two partners, in business as well as marriage, must be in accord about the essential purposes, if they are to have a harmonious relationship. In our culture where we select our own mates, it is during the courtship period that each person learns about the other's purposes. The courtship can fail to be beneficial in this, however, because insights about one another are often clouded over by infatuation. Goals must not be set aside because of one's glamour or charm. Purposes must not be overshadowed by personalities. Life's emphases must not be shelved for love's embracements.

The lack of mutual goals will produce a weak cleaving relationship, regardless of a powerful courtship. For example, Bill lives for sports events, while Barbara lives for the Savior. During the courtship she goes to the games with him and he goes to church with her. Neither one changes the emphasis in life. Both of them think, "I'll change him (her) when we marry." For a while after marriage, Bill and Barbara participate in the other's favorite activity, but trouble comes when their schedules conflict. The real conflict is not in programs but in people. Bill and Barbara live for two different reasons. The couple who stood hand in hand before the altar considers standing back to back before the judge. The things that appeared to be lasting—looks, personality, money, status—now take second place to the larger issues: goals and purposes.

Not only is agreement about goals necessary, but also agreement about the strategy to reach those goals. Jane and Jerry both want to live for God. Jane's strategy is activity within the community of believers, but Jerry's is through meditation in isolation. Soon their different ways will irritate each other, and they will begin to notice many other irritating characteristics in each other. These had been present during courtship, but now they become prominent. The "perfect couple" before the marriage has become a pitiful conflict after marriage.

The potential of many young people has been drained because of conflicts in goals, emphases, and strategies. A college student fails to communicate his dreams during the courtship period, to marry a partner who has different ambitions. As a result, some fantastic abilities have never been allowed to blossom. It is far worse to marry the wrong person than to stay single, even if one has the charisma, or desire, for marriage.

Even so, it is not enough to know about each other's life goals; two persons contemplating marriage must also know one another's characteristics. God designed marriage so that one person could complement another, or fill in where the other lacks. A happy selection therefore begins in knowing what you yourself lack and what you have to offer another person. This is not to say that a person should seek a mate who has opposite characteristics. Extreme opposites are seldom helpful to one another. If two extreme talkers should marry, chances are that neither will listen, and communication will suffer. If an extreme talker marries an extreme listener, only one-way communication takes place. If two extreme listeners marry, no one talks. No meaningful communication takes place, and the partners may isolate themselves from each other. Social and emotional problems can be seen down through the list.

The question in selecting a mate who will be a real helper is not just "Is he nice?" but "Is he necessary?" The criterion is not that "I can live with him," but "I cannot live without him." It is not only "I love him," but also "I need him."

What Should Be Done With In-laws?

Although a person leaves father and mother to marry, in a sense he takes them with him into the marriage. The couple brings to the new relationship many of the goals and views of life that were gained from the relationships with the parents. Also, to some extent, each accepts the view and way of life that were gained from the other's parents. It is important that both persons realize this fact. An illustration may help.

Bill's parents never emphasized special days, such as anniversaries or birthdays. In Barbara's home they were the cause for great celebration. Her father always gave her mother gifts for every occasion. On Barbara and Bill's first anniversary, Barbara prepares a candlelight dinner for Bill, as her mother always did for her father. Bill, as his father did, forgot all about their anniversary. Without considering how Bill was reared, Barbara could easily lash out in anger at Bill, believing he no longer loved her. In Bill's home, the only time his mother ever prepared a candlelight dinner was when she felt guilty about something. Without understanding how Barbara was reared, Bill could easily become suspicious as soon as he saw the table. Both partners need to take the time to understand each other and to develop their own life-style, for they have formed a new unit, a new family.

It may appear that the only way to have a happy marriage is for one to either marry a perfect person or at least learn all there is to know about the other before the wedding. However, a progressively happy marriage largely depends on the kind of person each is becoming, and the kind of person each is allowing the other to become. As each partner meets the needs of the other, they both grow and mature and are able to satisfy and be satisfied through marriage.

4

Love and Marriage

"Love and marriage, love and marriage
Go together like a horse and carriage;
Dad was told by Mother,
'You can't have one without the other.' "

This song is misleading in a sense, because it *is* possible to have one without the other. For instance, we certainly cannot marry every person of the opposite sex whom we love. Also, love is possible without marriage and marriage is possible without love. In many cultures this is the norm rather than the exception. In parent-arranged marriages, a bride and groom do not even meet until the wedding date is set. They may know about each other without knowing each other. Isaac and Rebekah experienced that type of marital beginning (Genesis 24).

Rather than love being the proper environment for marriage to grow, marriage is the proper environment for love to grow. Although love may not always lead to marriage, marriage must always lead to love. Love does not automatically create a new husband-wife unit. A husband-wife unit created by a marriage that involves leaving, cleaving, and unity creates the environment in which love can flourish.

This can be compared with children being born into a family. Their inclusion in the family initiates our love toward them. Our love for them as persons we know is not what makes them a part of the family. The same children born into another family would not call out that same kind of love from us. Their identification with the family, not their looks or abilities, elicits our love. So it is between a husband and wife. They belong to each other because of the marriage commitments they have made, and are to love each other out of that binding relationship. The marriage vows are a contract that binds.

The Bible considers marriage to be a covenant between two people, calling for the responsibility of faithfulness on the part of both (Malachi 2:14). Lack of love does not break the covenant. Our marriage vows do not read, "Until my love for you dies out." This interpretation is inherent in many marital relationships today. Thus, instead of our working at being faithful to the covenant commitment, we too often expect our mates to keep their love in high gear all the time. Then when love seems to wane, the marriage is over. Couples say, "We want to dissolve our marriage because we do not love each other anymore." This advice should be given to such a couple, "Then you had better begin to love each other."

Why is it that so often "love" seems to fail to sustain marriage? One reason may be that our society does not encourage couples to make a binding, unconditional commitment to each other. We are prone to stress independence, autonomy, individualism, and freedom rather than interpendence, community, or a corporate personality. Other factors must be considered also: the insecurity of our high mobility (people move often), the looseness of sexual expression outside marriage, the lack of interpersonal sharing, the glorification of freedom from marriage commitments (communicated through the mass media), and the lack of trust between people. The primary reason, however, is that, although we expect love to precede marriage, we know so little about mature love. Let us consider three different kinds of love. The Greeks called them *eros, philos*, and *agape*.

Eros is selfish love. When a person loves another just for personal gain, that is *eros*-love. It is only by coincidence if someone else is fulfilled or benefited. The other person's good is not considered. Some people call this the "I-love-you-if-you-do-such-and-such" or "if-you-love-me-you-will-do-such-and-such" kind of love. *Eros*-love enters a marriage with the determination to remain married only as long as things go well for self. Of course, this kind of love can never sustain a marriage. Run from *eros*-love! Do not think you can change it into a different kind of love after marriage. A person motivated by selfish love will not remain with you that long.

Philos is the "mutual-admiration-society" kind of love, such as the affection between two friends. It is a two-way love; it wants to receive as well as give. This appears to be marriage-sustaining, because it is an important kind of love. It is usually initiated by some likable quality one person sees in another. Thus it is based upon temporary characteristics of the two persons who are friends. This is sometimes called the "I-love-you-just-because" love. The person is loved because of beauty, agility at sports, intelligence, or other qualities. Although this kind of love is far superior to *eros*-love, it cannot sustain a marriage by itself. This is because the person loved in this way may lose that quality or characteristic, or someone else with a more appealing quality may come along.

Philos-love can foster suspicion and feelings of inferiority within a marriage. If a girl knows that her husband married her just because of her beauty, she may begin to worry and distrust him when she learns that a more beautiful girl works in his office. This kind of love can also foster dishonesty. If you realize that someone loves you just because of a certain characteristic, you may never allow that person to see other traits of your personality for fear he will not appreciate them. This sort of interplay prevents people from really knowing each other. The just-because love is too fickle to support a marriage.

Agape is unselfish love. It always lives for the well-being of another. It moves to meet the needs of another without counting the cost (never too high) or calculating the return (never too low). Some people call this the "I-love-you-in-spite-of" love. Coupled with *philos*-love it says, "I love you because of, and yet in spite of." This means, "There are reasons I have fallen in love with you, but now my love goes deeper than those initial reasons. If those reasons should no longer exist, I love you as a person in spite of it. Now it is the total you I love with my total self."

This kind of love is self-giving. It invests and gives oneself to another. The more we love like this, the more we initiate the same kind of love from the other person. *Agape*-love destroys the idea that marriage is a fifty-fifty proposition. A fifty-fifty deal creates difficulties, for it says, "I will go only halfway to meet your needs." This attitute withholds the self and weakens the cleaving relationship. It hampers a meeting, for who knows where the halfway point is? To come short means there will be no meeting point at all. *Agape*-love solves this dilemma, for it says, "I will go all the way to meet your needs." If both husband and wife are determined to do this, the two will meet in harmony. The exact meeting point of the give-and-take may vary, but the willingness to give never varies. There should always be that willingness for total giving, not for total taking.

The characteristics of *agape*-love are diverse, yet are unified in one principle, that of living for the good of the other. This love begins with an acceptance of God's love in Jesus Christ and a response of love to God. When we realize that God loves us, we can love ourselves. Then we can love others, for our love is always conditioned by how we accept ourselves. If we are uneasy with ourselves, we will be uneasy with others. If we do not trust ourselves, we will not trust others. If we feel inferior, we will say and do things to make someone else feel inferior. If we are not honest with ourselves, we will not be honest with another.

Jesus touched on this concept when He taught that the greatest commandment is to love God, and the second greatest is to love others as oneself (Matthew 22:37-39). We must accept God's love for us and accept ourselves. Only then can we take on the humbling attitude of a servant toward another. When we have accepted ourselves, we do not have to build up ourselves or protect ourselves with defense mechanisms. We are free to extend ourselves in another's life, free to receive both criticism and compliments from the other.

Christ died for us so that God's Spirit of love, who gives us the ability to love God and accept self, will live in us. This is the Spirit of freedom, releasing us from the slavery of selfishness, which is the essence of sin. We are now free to live for God (Romans 6:6-11; 2 Corinthians 5:15). This freedom allows us to regard others with a different perspective (2 Corinthians 5:16). We are free to be servants (v. 18). "Free to serve" appears contradictory, but it is not, for service is the characteristic of God's love. Man was made in God's likeness. To be freed, then, is to be unfettered from whatever hinders us from living in accordance with our created nature: the unselfishness of God's character. That freedom is initially expressed by humble evaluation of self: "I bid every one among you not to think of himself more highly than he ought to think" (Romans 12:3). This advice comes after eleven chapters of Paul's developing the theme of God's acceptance of us. He put it this way, "In humility count others better than yourselves" (Philippians 2:3). No gender is attached to this. It is a mandate for all Christians. Husbands and wives must look at each other with this perspective. Neither male chauvinism nor women's lib must be allowed to foster feelings of superiority. "Let each of you look not only to his own interests, but also to the interests of others" (v. 4). We are not to reach for a superior status, but for a servant's stance (vv. 5-8). Through a servant's stance Christ was fulfilled and exalted (v. 9), and so it is with us who are made and remade in His likeness (Ephesians 4:22-24).

This kind of living should begin at home. This is why, after two tremendous teachings listing the characteristics of love, Paul immediately applied them to the husband-wife relationship (Ephesians 4:22—5:23). These characteristics are necessary for marriage. Let us consider some of them.

Put away falsehood. Speak the truth to one another. Husbands and wives need to be open with each other. Neither can really know the other if either one wears a mask. Truthfulness is related to one's being trustworthy. If you want your husband or wife to trust you, be truthful.

Be angry, but do not sin. Do not let the sun set upon your anger. The husband and wife need to communicate their differences. Anger over any issue should not be carried over to the next day, never! If it is, the devil will take advantage of it by bringing disunity into the home. That is why Paul immediately says, "And give no opportunity to the devil" (v. 27).

Do not steal from each other. Both husband and wife should contribute their energies to the livelihood of the family according to the roles of each. Each should recognize how the other is needed for the family. Neither should be lazy and sponge off the other.

Mind your tongue. Speech should build up each other; therefore speak well of each other and to each other. Replace slander with kindness. Remember that belittling each other whittles away the cleaving relationship. Words affect the total being of a person. Careless or unkind words can break a person's spirit and even his health, while kind and encouraging words can build him up (Proverbs 12:18). Our speech at home should help maintain the unity of the home.

Mind your attitude. Grudges and bitterness should

be replaced with forgiveness. A willingness to talk over grievances and work out the difficulties will go far to replace such attitudes as sullenness, bad temper, or stubbornness. Many admit, "I'll forgive, but I won't forget." Deciding to remember hampers forgiveness and keeps the grudges just around the corner. A person must develop the ability to forget. You can forget anything you want to forget. Merely forgetting, however, is not necessarily forgiving. Just forgetting may not be a positive activity, but a neglectful one. Just forgetting calls for no mutual reacceptance of one another. Only as the offender and the one offended together condemn the wrong, decide to forget it, and walk together without hostility, does forgiveness take place. Then alienation of a couple is replaced by reconciliation.

This discussion of the characteristics is summed up in Ephesians 4:30: "Do not grieve the Holy Spirit." To avoid grieving the Holy Spirit, we must walk by the Spirit of God whom we have received (Galatians 5:25). This means that each person is to manifest the fruit of the Spirit as listed in Galatians 5:22-24. These kinds of interpersonal relationships are to begin at home between husband and wife. They spotlight the truth of Ephesians 5:21, which says that each is to submit to the other. Submission is not the role of the wife only, but also the husband. Submission means the voluntary giving up of selfish interests for the well-being of another.

Agape-love will revolutionize every dimension of a marriage. It will free a person to function as a helper fit for another. Applied by both husband and wife, it will revolutionize their life-style—how the leisure time of both will be lived, how reactions are expressed, how the future is anticipated, and how the present is filled. It will affect even the intimate sexual expression of the husband and wife, for each is living to please the other in this important aspect of marriage.

How Will I Know I'm in Love?

We have seen how the right kind of love is necessary for the stability of a marriage and the security of individuals within the marriage. Since in our culture love usually precedes marriage, it is very important that before marriage a person is able to recognize the right kind of love. This is especially true today when so many couples think it is time to dissolve the marriage when love is missing.

When I am counseling engaged couples, the conversation goes something like this:

"Why do you want to marry each other?"

"Because we love each other."

"How do you know you love each other?"

Profound silence! I get the impression that each is inwardly asking, "How *do* I know?" Then, after a long pause, the answer is usually, "We like to be together."

Now, that is nice; however, there are many people I like to be with, but I don't want to marry them. It is one thing to like to be with someone when most of the conditions are favorably planned and executed. It is quite another to live together when the pay check stops, the baby is vomiting, the toddler is crying, the wife or the husband is sick in bed, one or the other is out of sorts, or the plumbing is frozen. How can two persons know in advance that their love can survive small crises such as these? There are times in a marriage when the husband and wife simply do not like being together. A marriage resting upon that foundation alone would be shaky indeed.

Love is not such a nonemotional reality that we can create a complete list to be checked off (as a pilot does) to know whether or not we are ready for a takeoff in marriage. At the same time, certain considerations during courtship can be valuable.

1. Read the New Testament teachings about the husband-wife relationships and compare them with

your relationship during courtship. Ladies, is the husband-to-be a decision-maker? Does he love you as Christ loves the church? That is, is he willing to sacrifice for you? Can he forfeit self-interests for you? Can you do the same for him? Can he serve you? Is he concerned about your spiritual welfare? Does he act like a drill sergeant, expecting you to obey (Ephesians 5:25-33)? Is he harsh with you (Colossians 3:19)? Is he considerate of you? Does he honor you as a woman, or does he belittle you (1 Peter 3:7)? Can you be submissive to him (Colossians 3:18)? Check your relationship against Paul's teaching (1 Corinthians 13; Galatians 5:22-26; Ephesians 4: Colossians 3). This is not calling for perfection before marriage, but for maturity. These characteristics cannot belong to a person who is not a Christian.

2. Is there not only a feeling of pleasure but also of respect for the person? *Agape* love is not identified by a tingling feeling when two people touch. A tingle is the sign of life, not love. Our physical chemistry produces a feeling of pleasure when the opposite sexes touch, but real love balances this feeling with respect for the other. *Agape*-love will not desecrate the other person for selfish pleasure, as *eros*-love will. When a boy says, "If you love me, you will let me—" the girl can reply, "If you love me, you will never put me in a position to answer you until we are married." *Agape*-love is a self-giving love. This does not refer to a giving of one's body in a sexual act before marriage, but of being unselfish and undemanding. It combines happiness with humility. In fact, giving oneself involves the denial of one kind of self-interest for another—an interest and esteem in the other as a person of God. The dates could include the prayer that God's will be done and that they will glorify Him.

3. *Agape*-love revolves around the total person, not just one aspect of a person. To test this, one should consider what his own response would be if the initial

attraction that drew his affection were threatened. For instance, men, if you were drawn to her by her beauty, what would happen if you caught her sometime with her make-up off and her hair in curlers? Women, if you were drawn to him by his activities in church, what about his behavior in other activities? How does he or she act toward others? Can joy be combined with concern for another's good? If you know each other in only one environment (college campus, for instance), observe her or him in another, such as the home, for a few days. Observe the person in that setting. Chances are the person will transfer much of his behavior in that environment to the new home life. Do not lend a deaf ear to those people who have close contact with the one you are thinking of marrying. Listen to what they say about him or her. Remember that you are to love the entire person forever, not just the attractive or exciting aspects.

In evaluating premarital love, do not seek to change the other person nor expect perfection. Do consider whether or not you can love that person as is, even if he or she never changes. Think of that! There will always be differences between husband and wife, but *agape*-love handles those differences. It does not demand conformity, but fosters unity amid diversity, without animosity. Since this self-giving love binds everything together (Colossians 3:14), you can build a marriage on it. It will permit you and your mate to stay together during difficult or disagreeable times. How do you know you are in love? When the love compares favorably with the love that Jesus has for you.

5

"Till Death Do Us Part"

Divorce and remarriage are not twentieth-century inventions. Jesus stepped into our history at a time when they were common commodities. The alienation was clearly seen in the fences people built to separate themselves from others who were different—race, class, sex, health, religion, politics. It was also seen in the fragmentation within the home.

Seneca, an historian of that time, said that people divorced to remarry, and married to get divorced. He observed that some of the people identified the years, not by the names of the emperors, but by the names of their wives or husbands of that year. On one occasion, Jesus met a woman who had had five husbands, and was not married to the man with whom she was then living (John 4).

The Jews looked for ways to participate in these activities without violating God's law. Rather than rest upon God's initial announcement about marriage in Genesis 2:24, and ignoring Moses' commandment, they looked to Moses' later allowance for divorce: ''When a man takes a wife and marries her, if then she finds no favor in his eyes because he has found some indecency in her, and he writes her a bill of divorce—'' (Deuteronomy 24:1). Some fanciful interpretative footwork danced around that verse to justify divorce and remarriage.

The chief question centered around the word ''indecency.'' When is a wife indecent so that she can be divorced? One school of Jewish thought (Shammai) said that only adultery was indecent and thus constituted the only ground for divorce and remarriage. Another school of thought (Rabbi Hillel) said that anything the husband did not like was indecent, since the wife lived to please the husband. The words "she finds no favor in his eyes" defined indecency. Thus the husband could divorce her if she burned his food, spoke to another man in public, wore her hair down in public, said anything bad about her in-laws, or was less beautiful than another woman. It was belief and practice of this kind that prompted Jesus to teach that men should stop divorcing their wives (Matthew 5:32; Luke 16:18). He challenged the rabbis' attitude about women. He talked with women in public, trusted, praised, and helped them.

The two competing schools of thought about divorce give us the Jewish environment to which Jesus spoke and Paul wrote. (Read and study Matthew 5:31, 32; 19:1-12; Mark 10:2-12; Luke 16:18; Romans 7:2, 3; 1 Corinthians 7:10-16, 39, 40.) There are four basic interpretations or understandings of the New Testament teaching concerning divorce and remarriage.

1. Some understand that Jesus' teachings permit an "innocent" person to remarry, if the mate has severed a marriage by committing adultery. Matthew 5:32 and 19:9 are cited as "permissive" texts.

2. In addition to adultery being a Biblical ground for divorce and remarriage, some understand that Paul permits a Christian to remarry, if he or she has been deserted by a non-Christian mate (1 Corinthians 7:10-16).

3. Another view is that the Scriptural grounds for divorce and remarriage are much broader than the first two positions. Although God's ideal is that marriage be binding until death separates the two, many cannot receive this ideal. If the two partners cannot live in peace, God will not force this ideal upon them. The last sentence in 1 Corinthians 7:15, "But God hath called us to peace," and Matthew 19:11, "All men cannot receive this saying," are combined and used to support this position. Some penetrating questions are

36

put forth by those persons who take this position:

Does God really expect a wife, perhaps living with a drunkard who habitually beats her and the children, to remain bound to him until he commits adultery?

What if he has absolutely no interest in sex, and mistreats his wife in every other way?

Can "adultery" refer to something broader than just a physical act? Can it refer to failure to live for another, as it was used by the Lord to describe Israel?

4. The fourth view is that a Christian is given permission to remarry only if his mate has died, and even then to only another Christian. Those who hold this position believe that the "exception" clause in Matthew 5:32 relates to the responsibility for the adultery. They feel that Jesus was saying that the husband by divorcing his wife will be responsible for the adultery she commits by remarrying, except if she has committted adultery before the divorce. In that case, she will bear the full responsibility.

The popularly accepted text in Matthew 19:9 does permit remarriage after divorce, if adultery is the issue; however, those with this understanding rightly observe that this reading may not be the original, since other ancient Greek manuscripts of Matthew do not permit remarriage after divorce. They read this way: "Whoever divorces his wife, except for immorality, makes her commit adultery; and he who marries a divorced woman commits adultery." Some scholars note that this reading agrees with the teachings of Jesus and Paul. Also note that the disciples' reaction to Jesus' statement of Matthew 19:9 does not read as though they understood it as Jesus giving permission.

Those who hold this last position are correct to note that the word "bondage" in 1 Corinthians 7:15 is not the same as "bound," which Paul used in 7:39 and Romans 7:2. The word used in 1 Corinthians 7:15 describes the situation of one person's serving another. It is a functional word. The word in 7:39 and Romans

7:2 describes a legal binding of two persons. Is Paul then saying that, if a non-Christian mate leaves a Christian mate, the Christian mate does not have the responsibility to continually meet some needs of the other, such as sex? The context of 1 Corinthians 7:2-7 lends weight to this understanding of "not under bondage" in verse 15. Is Paul saying that one is positionally a wife (7:39) but not one functionally (7:15), if the unbelieving partner decides to leave? The issue is certainly complex, with different understandings possible. Some teachings are clear:

1. It was God's original intention that only death sever a marriage (Genesis 2:24; Matthew 19:5, 6; Mark 10:6-9; Romans 7:2, 3; 1 Corinthians 7:39).

2. Moses allowed divorce on the ground of independency because of the insensitivity of the people (Deuteronomy 24; Matthew 19:7, 8; Mark 10:3-6).

3. Reconciliation or remaining unmarried after divorce are the ideals (1 Corinthians 7:10, 11).

4. Jesus never condemned anyone because of his present marital status (John 4).

Christians probably will continue to hold diverse views about this issue until the Lord returns. Each must continue to study and to allow his personal position to rest upon the teachings and understanding of God's Word, rather than our experiences in the traditions of the world. We must also relate to fellow Christians who hold positions that differ from ours. We must do this in the character of Christ and with His willingness to minister to a person regardless of his status in life. An appeal to Jesus for remarriage after divorce rests more upon His love, mercy, grace, and forgiveness than upon the "permissive" texts.

Why does marriage have such a high standard in God's design? Why are divorce and remarriage not obvious options? Because of the major reasons for marriage. Creating the sexes was one of God's ways to fill in where we lack and thus help each of us reach our maximum potential. That is why, after the first marriage. God said His creation was *very* good (Genesis 1:31).

Separation from our mates, on the other hand, hinders us from maturing properly. In divorce our personal needs are not met. Some will reply, "But my needs were not met in marriage either." If that is so, it is because the couple did not apply the principle of cleaving, or did not live out their respective roles. A marriage creates such a unit that to love your mate is to love yourself (Ephesians 5:28). To cut off your mate is to cut off something of yourself. So it was out of Jesus' love for us that He said, "Whom God has yoked together, no man must separate."

Divorce in the Church

As we realize that God did not intend for a marriage to be broken, many questions come to our minds concerning people in the church who have been involved in divorce. If an innocent person is divorced and remarried, what is he to do? What if a person is married to a divorcee? If a person is divorced, does he have to remain single the rest of his life? Can a person be a mature Christian and be divorced? Should the church accept divorced people for membership? Can a divorced person work in the church?

I believe we should follow Jesus' example. First, we should recognize that Moses' concession about divorce did not square with God's design in creating marriage; however, God did not directly intervene with Moses' concession. Second, we should teach with clarity that divorce and remarriage are not God's intention and that He is not pleased with it. Third, we should not condemn those who have been divorced and are remarried. We must teach with the hope of affecting the future decisions people may make. Past decisions have been made and little can be done to reverse them. Our word must prevent, not condemn.

We have often failed to differentiate between prevention and condemnation. We seem to think that while we teach that divorce is not within God's original intention, we must also condemn those who have been divorced. Jesus did not do this! Paul did not do this! Besides the occasion in John 4, Jesus was also confronted with the situation of a woman caught in the very act of adultery. Jesus stood with her against her accusers with a forgiving word when others were ready to stone her.

Neither was a divorced person prevented from being a candidate for church membership in the first two centuries of Christianity, nor was a person excommunicated if he became divorced. This does not mean that divorce was sanctioned by the church, but that the church was ministering to people's real needs. The church demonstrated the possibility of a future with God, regardless of the past. We must not forget that there is only one unforgiveable sin, and it is *not* divorce and remarriage.

Our God is a forgiving and an accepting God. The meaning of grace emphasizes His lovingkindness, His favor to us, His acceptance of us, and His granting to us what we do not deserve. God is not in the practice of accepting those who have made only perfect decisions in the past. He does not accept us or forgive us on the basis of our worth, but on the basis of our faith and love to Him. Whatever marital situation you find yourself in, decide to devote the rest of your life to pleasing God. Leave the past to His grace. The most important influence of life is not so much how we have traveled in the past as it is in the direction in which we are now headed.

Let us now consider the questions more specifically. If a person is divorced and remarried, what should he do? Of course, the ideal situation is for reconciliation with the first mate, but that would be impractical, since another marriage has been entered, and perhaps even two. He should therefore repent and ask God's blessing upon his life, then receive God's acceptance and forgiveness. Let him remain married and dedicate the present and future to God.

Does a person who is divorced and not remarried have to remain single? That arrangement fits God's intention best (1 Corinthians 7:10, 11). To remarry is to hamper a possible reconciliation. Who knows what God may work out of an ugly situation? Jesus faced the ugliest situation possible, but God brought victory and beauty out of it because Jesus could pray, "If thou be willing, remove this cup from me: nevertheless not my will, but thine, be done" (Luke 22:42). We also must pray that God's will be done.

Some may say, "It is too cruel to expect a divorcee to remain single, especially if he or she is an innocent party." Is this severity too hard in the light of the levity that so many exercise in deciding whether or not to marry and to whom? Some people are going to have to display the courage to bear the brunt of this severity, if our society, especially youth, is to learn about the seriousness of entering a marriage contract.

Shouldn't we recognize the fact that society has helped foster an attitude of levity about marriage? Young people are pressured to marry by a certain age. The difficulties of our own marriages are hidden from our children, so they grow up believing that marriage is always one happy dream. We do this as we glorify multiple marriages of the heroes and stars of the mass media. We do this as we laugh at jokes about marriage. We do this as we watch programs and movies that spotlight the lack of commitment in marriage. We do this as we allow *Playboy* and *Cosmopolitan* to be read in our homes.

Although Christians may not be able to turn the tide of all society, they should be committed to living out God's intentions regardless of the surrounding cultural norms. Our children must see more of a demonstration

of God's intentions. This may call for individual hard-
ships, but that is a lesser evil than the breakdown of
the stability of marriage, which in turn weakens society.

Can a divorced person be a mature Christian? Of
course! Should the church accept divorced-remarried
persons for membership? Of course! Should a divorced person work in the church? Of course! Every
Christian has charisma (gift or ability) for work in the
church (Romans 12; 1 Corinthians 12), and each
member is to be involved in some work of the ministry
(Ephesians 4:7, 11, 12, 16). Christian divorced persons
are members of the family of God the same as other
Christians.

Should a divorced person be a leader in the church?
Of course! Leadership is not a role we elect. It is a role
one lives. Some leaders are never elected into leadership "slots." Others who are elected as leaders are not
leaders. Each congregation will have to decide about
the qualifications of elders and deacons, based upon
the statement, "husband of one wife" (1 Timothy 3:2,
12). Remember, however, that the other qualifications
are just as important. "The husband of one wife" is
not the major criterion. Many congregations will not
allow the nomination of a divorced man who fills all
the other qualifications, but do allow a married man
who may not be apt to teach, may not be hospitable,
and may be quarrelsome. I do not think we should
water down any of the qualifications, nor elevate any.
Most congregations need to consider the functions of
the elders and deacons before considering their qualifications. Anyone can serve the Communion and col-
lect the offering. Those are hardly the functions exclu-
sively reserved for elders and deacons.

Let us live within the family of God with the love of
God toward each other. Let us be determined to build
up one another, not to tear down each other. Let us
develop the forgiving attitude of God himself. Let us

teach a preventive word with conviction and clarity, so that we may allow God's Word to be effective in stopping the present trend of irresponsibility about marriage. May our children learn the intention of God and so be committed to follow that intention when they marry. May levity give way to seriousness. Let us stop the condemning words, but minister to one another so that we all may grow up in every way into Him who is our head—Christ.

The Ministry of the Church to the Divorced

A divorce is a traumatic experience for all persons concerned. Christians should be sensitive to the needs that divorcees have and meet those needs. In many ways, family members face similar needs following a separation by divorce to those following a separation by death. There is often shock, failure to accept the reality, grief, loneliness, and guilt. There is often a living in the past and a reluctance to adjust to home, community, career, and church responsibilities. Christians should minister to these needs without taking sides. Remember, there is seldom, if ever, an "innocent" party in any divorce. What can Christians do to minister to divorced persons? Here are some suggestions in meeting their needs:

Socially. Keep the lines of communication open by writing, telephoning, or visiting. Avoid discussing the situation at home or with others. Allow the divorcee to contribute ideas and let her feel these are appreciated. Never compare the person's situation with another situation you know. Invite the person into your home. Bring the children and yours together for social fun.

Practically. If the divorcee is a woman, offer help or suggestions with business affairs, house repairs, the automobile, etc. If the divorcee is a man, offer help with the housekeeping tasks, training of his daughters, etc. If financial help is needed, this will require unselfish sharing. A Parents Without Partners Club could be formed, with practical needs of the divorced in mind.

For the children. Husband-wife teams could teach Sunday-school classes and be youth sponsors. Men in the church could include the boys in masculine activities, such as fishing, hunting, hiking, camping, carpentry. Women in the church could include the girls in feminine activities, such as cooking, sewing, decorating, gardening, shopping.

In the church, Divorced people need the church, and the church needs them. The minister should offer post-divorce counseling to discover potential problem areas, and then he and/or other members of the church should minister to them in those areas. Encourage the person to attend as many functions of the church as he or she did before. Make personal visits to assure the person of continued welcome and of continued love as a Christian brother or sister. Share with divorced persons the love and acceptance of God. Help them feel accepted, especially if guilt feelings are present. Include them in class discussions, and involve them in congregational activities, offering opportunities to serve others. Discover their abilities and use them.

Decisions of the Divorced

There are several decisions that the divorced person can make to help the broken home become a happier place. Here are some suggestions:

Stay involved in the church.

Read the Bible regularly. Read a New Testament book through each day for thirty days, selecting a different book each month. Another method is to count the pages in your New Testament and divide by 30, and the number of pages in your Old Testament by 180. Determine to read that number of pages each day, alternating between the Testaments. Either way, you will become saturated by the Word of God.

Do not blame yourself or others. If you were wrong, even partially, admit it, condemn the wrong, forget it, and live with the forgiveness of God from this point.

Do not stop communicating with your friends because you think they won't accept you.

Never waste time wondering and worrying about what others are thinking.

Organize your time so that you can fit in the tasks the missing mate took care of.

Never criticize your former mate in front of the children. Do not make them feel they caused the divorce, or force them into a position of choosing between the parents.

Spend time with the children. Help them develop their special abilities. They need you; do not let them lose both parents. Check on activities that you can do with the children and that do not cost much: zoos, museums, free concerts, amusement parks, school activities. Carry out formerly made plans, such as vacations.

Do not "crawl in a hole." Invite your close friends to visit with you soon. If you need advice, turn to someone whom you trust and respect. Plan some time for yourself without the children.

Do not "let yourself go," mentally or physically. Go to the beauty parlor regularly. Shop for new clothes occasionally. If you cannot drive, take lessons. Do not overuse the television as an escape. Subscribe to a daily newspaper and keep current. Begin a habit of reading good books and listening to good music. Subscribe to and read at least one good Christian periodical. If at all possible, take a college course, audit one (no assignments), or consider taking a Bible college correspondence course.

Do not glorify or despise your divorced status.

While a divorce brings great losses to a home, it need not destroy the persons in the home. Jesus never said or implied that a home which suffers a divorce cannot be a happy one. It can, but it takes His help and the ministry of the church.

6

The Cement of a Marriage

Getting married is becoming easier than joining the Marines, but enlistment in the Marines sometimes begins a more lasting and binding relationship than marriage does. Often two persons united in marriage clash head-on over trivial matters and give up. Why? An "expectation gap" is one villain. The husband enters marriage with certain expectations about his own role and that of his wife. The wife also enters the marriage with certain expectations about their respective roles.

There are sound reasons why these expectations do not agree. Each person was reared in a different family, with different life-styles. Each has read different books and dreamed different dreams. The man may enter marriage expecting to be the only breadwinner, while the wife expects to continue her career. On the other hand, the husband may expect the wife to help with the expenses, while she expects to be a homemaker only. The wife may expect her husband to help her with the dishes, just as her father always helped her mother. The man may never expect to touch a dish, except to eat out of it.

Marriage creates a glued-together unit, but that unit is made up of two individuals who could begin to pull apart. Uncommunicated expectations can weaken the glue of the cleaving relationship of marriage. What can keep the two differing persons together? How can they function as a unit amid such wide differences? Only as they accept and apply God's will for each member of the family. God never intended for members of a family to live in continuous contention and competition, neglectful of the other's needs.

Within the context of discussing marriage, Paul

wrote, "God hath called us to peace" (1 Corinthians 7:15). Peace means the absence of alienation, but how does peace reign in a family? It can reign only as the Prince of peace lives within the husband and wife, and only as each gives in to God's will for the family. When the Prince of peace enters our lives, we are reconciled to God *and* to each other, regardless of external differences (Ephesians 2:14-22). The family can function as a unit only as the husband and wife belong to a larger unit—the family of God. The husband and wife in Christ become new creatures (2 Corinthians 5:17, equipped to live unselfishly (v. 15), with a new perspective about others (v. 16). They become ministers of reconciliation (v. 18), not masters of war. Intrafamily war erupts from the same source as international war—selfish desire (James 4).

Only as husband and wife become new creatures united with God's kind of characteristics (John 14:15-21; Acts 2:38) can they live the unselfish, unassuming life that is necessary in a family. For this reason Paul preceded his advice about family living (Ephesians 5:22-33; Colossians 3:18 ff.) with a discussion about unity with Christ (Ephesians 2; Colossians 2:9, 10) and the characteristics needed to maintain that unity (Ephesians 4:17—5:20; Colossians 3).

Paul gave us the blueprint for success in marital roles. Spiritual righteousness precedes success in these roles, for they require the right kind of persons. People cannot merely read a book about husband-wife roles or attend lectures and then assume the roles. The passages in the Bible that concern marital roles is not a course in sociology, but a concern for spirituality.

The Spirit of Christ is the cement that keeps the cleaving relationship together. The first fruit of the Spirit is love (Galatians 5:22), and love binds everything together in perfect harmony (Colossians 3:15). Neither Paul nor Peter wrote about the roles of husband and wife to just people in general, but to Christians in particular. The advice in Ephesians and Colossians was written to the saints (Ephesians 1:1; Colossians 1:2). Peter's advice was written to those who had been sanctified by the Spirit (1 Peter 1:2). Only the person who has God's nature participating in him can function with God's characteristics. His characteristics, lived out, secure a marriage.

From the beginning, man was created to share God's life. God shared himself with the first man at two levels—His character and activities. He shared His character with man when He breathed into man the "breath of life" (Genesis 2:7). That "breath of life" was God's life (His Spirit). Thus man was created in God's own image (1:27). That image equipped man to share in God's activities. God called man to participate in creating, in domineering (1:28), and in caring (2:15). As long as man remained open to the resources of God's life within, he lived a life of cooperation with God, himself, his mate, and nature.

Adam and Eve decided to rebel against being partners under God by seeking to be persons equal to God. Their sin was the determination to make decisions apart from God's will. That determination caused them to lose God's inner life (3:3). The death they died was separation from God's character (Isaiah 59:2). After that separation, they did not function as God intended, but were at one another's throats. Harmony was replaced by harshness. While God's Spirit had brought order out of chaos (Genesis 1:2), the first husband and wife brought chaos into order. Nowhere is this more vividly seen than in the interpersonal breakdown in the family relationships. In the largest family unit, the family of God, the man and wife hid from the Creator-Father and tried to deceive Him. In the smaller family unit, husband and wife, open communication and sharing gave way to blame-throwing. Adam's excitement on his wedding day,

"This is at last bone of my bones," gave way to disappointment, "The woman You gave me" (Genesis 3:12). How often today does the glow of the wedding day dim rather than brighten as the anniversaries come? Without the Spirit of God abiding in the members, a family cannot express the trust, love, and peace that keeps alienation replaced by acceptance.

The Old Testament is filled with stories that show families in trouble. The first child born on this earth murdered the second child (Genesis 4). Within seven generations, the beauty of marriage was marred by bigamy (4:19). Violence eventually filled the earth (6:13). God decided to make a new start for humanity, and He began it through another family. This did not mean that humanity would henceforth have ideal family relationships. We could go on through the Old Testament, spotlighting many kinds of family difficulties. But what is the solution to such problems? The coming of the Messiah would make it possible for God's Spirit to live again in the lives of people (Jeremiah 31:31 ff.; Ezekiel 11:19; 36:26, 37). He will make that possible by taking our sins, which separate us from God's Spirit, into himself as if He had sinned, and offering us what is left: reconciliation with God's Spirit. Although He never sinned (Hebrews 4:15), Jesus became sin so that we could become righteous (2 Corinthians 5:21). God laid all our sins upon Him (Isiah 53:6). On the cross Jesus tasted our death for us (Hebrews 2:9), the death of separation from God, the death that sin brings (Isaiah 59:2; Romans 6:23). God forgave our sins in Jesus' death, leaving His body sinless. Then God's Spirit reentered His body and Jesus arose by the Spirit (Acts 2:24; Romans 8:11).

Through God's gracious love our sins are forgiven in Jesus. When we accept that forgiveness we receive the gift of the Holy Spirit (Acts 2:38), and arise to walk in a new quality of life (Romans 6). The image of God has been restored in us (Ephesians 4:24; Colossians

3:9). We are new creatures (2 Corinthians 5:17) because God's character has been renewed in us through the Holy Spirit (Titus 3:5).

We are now free to live the unselfish kind of life that God lives (Romans 15:3; 2 Corinthians 5:15), because we have been reunited with God (Ephesians 2:16). But that is not all; we are also united with our mate who is a Christian. In Christ the dividing walls of hostility are broken down (v. 14). A husband and wife can now walk together in Christ, for they share the same kind of life. The way the family of God will live together in Heaven can begin on earth within the families of men.

The new life in Christ liberates us to serve one another in love (Galatians 5:13, 22-24). The first fruit of the Spirit is *love* (agape-love), followed by *joy*, that kind of buoyance which comes from being accepted by God and living a life of accepting others. *Peace* follows, then comes *patience*, which means putting up with one another. Oh, how that is needed in the husband-wife relationship! Patience opens the door for *kindness*, that sweet attitude which expresses itself in doing what is for the other's good. *Trustworthiness* is an important part of marriage, in the performing of the separate functions of the unit. *Gentleness* is needed when difficulties arise, going hand in hand with *self-control*, which manifests itself in the mastery of inner attitudes as well as desires and ambitions.

These qualities are from God, and will be the normal life-style within His family in Heaven. He has made that same life-style available for earthly families as well, for "those who belong to Jesus Christ have crucified the flesh with its lusts and desires" (Galatians 5:24). Those in Christ utilize the Spirit (Romans 8:13). The closer a husband and wife are to God, the closer they are to each other. When they are filled with God's Spirit, they are perfectly united. To be filled with the Spirit does not mean that we have more of the Spirit, but the Spirit has more of us.

To quench the Spirit is to live contrary to the life of the Spirit. It is to retaliate, to have wrong inclinations, to be in constant despair, to neglect prayer (1 Thessalonians 5:16-22). To grieve the Spirit is to live in opposition to the fruits of the Spirit—in short, living in the *un*-likeness of God.

It was certainly by a deliberate plan that Paul preceded the activities of the marital roles with the facts of the Master's reconciliation. Thus, the question that each must ask before considering the marital roles themselves is this: "Am I the right kind of person? Am I a new creature in Christ? Am I free to live and give unselfishly? Is the image of God living in me? Are my attitudes His, so that His way for the family will be mine?"

If the answers to these questions are negative, the husband will not be able to love his wife as Christ loved the church (Ephesians 5:25). Neither will a wife be able to submit to her husband as to the Lord (Ephesians 5:22). If there were any possible formula other than abiding in Christ, He would not have died for us. He would have merely outlined the roles for us.

Are you a Christ-filled person? If not, how do you think your family can be the unit God intended? Do you want it to be? If so, become the right person by putting on Christ (Romans 13:14; 2 Corinthians 5:17; Galatians 3:27). Accept the right basis for a successful marriage as both a partner of God and complement to your mate. This is not only preparation for assuming the right roles within a marriage, but it is an exciting, abundant way to live.

7

Family Roles Introduced

How many members are in a Christian family? A Christian family has a minimum of three: God, the husband, and the wife. It has a maximum of six different categories of members: God, the husband, wife, children, relatives who live in, and pets. Each of these has a specific role to be expressed within the family.

God in the Family

God instituted the family unit as an expression of His love for us. Because the Maker of man knew what man needed for his greatest good and pleasure, God provided the means to meet those needs. The family is one of God's special provisions for man. Long before we heard it from sociologists, we read it in the Bible: the family is man's primary group for fulfilling his basic needs and providing the environment for his development as a personality.

One of God's revelations about the family is that He is to have first place in the home. Respect for God is listed at the head of the Ten Commandments. Jesus reemphasized this by saying, "He that loveth father or mother more than me is not worthy of me: and he that loveth son or daughter more than me is not worthy of me" (Matthew 10:37). In Luke 14:26, He said the same thing in another way: "If any man come to me, and hate not his father, and mother, and wife, and children, and brethren, and sisters, yea, and his own life also, he cannot be my disciple." Jesus was not speaking harshly. He was not saying that we should despise family members or ourselves. He also taught that we should honor father and mother (Matthew 15:4-6) and have a cleaving relationship with the marriage partner (Matthew 19:5). He also made it clear that we are to love each other (Matthew 22:39). Jesus certainly did not contradict himself, but gave us priorities by which we can love others properly.

The Greek word for "hate" in Luke 14:26 means to give someone second place. Jesus said that we should put our love for family members beneath our love for Him. As we share our love first with God, He will share His love with us. It is as His love abides in us that we are better able to love others (John 15; Romans 5:5; 1 John 4:16). He who abides in love abides in God (1 John 4:16). Although love begins with God, it cannot end there (1 John 4:21).

If we bypass or neglect devotion and love to God in order to show more love for the family, we will deplete our love capacity. Love that puts God anywhere but in first place will not last through wealth and poverty, sickness and health, agreements and disagreements. Only when God is the honored guest in our hearts will the home survive tensions.

Pets

The subject of pets is mentioned early in order to set it aside quickly. In some homes pets are treated as the most important members of the family. People need to express love, and if they are threatened by intimate association with another person or have lost respect for another person, they may transfer love from a person to a pet. For some people, loving property instead of people is a way of life. Despite all the bad about the ancient city of Sodom, one thing was praiseworthy: the king of Sodom valued people over property (Genesis 14:21).

When the husband comes home and pets the dog before he kisses his wife, it is little wonder that the dog's tail wags while the wife's spirit drags. God created man to have dominion over animals (1:28) and to love the mate (2:24). It is a perversion of God's intention to love the mongrel and dominate the mate.

God's design for marriage is centered on the cleaving relationship (2:24). Nothing should come between what God has glued together. Whenever one mate begins to stick to a pet, the other is no longer the center of his life. The husband-wife relationship will be weakened. Some people may say, "We are closer to each other because of the pet we mutually love." The problem with that thinking is that God, not a pet, should draw the husband and wife closer together. If the pet is substituted as a unifying agent, what happens to the togetherness when it is gone? A pet is only temporary. God must be the uniting factor. He is eternal!

Relatives Who Live In

Having parents or other adult relatives living in the home can be either a delightful or a dreadful experience, depending upon the attitudes of those involved. Married children must realize that these relatives need to be treated with dignity. They are not to be treated as adopted children or as permanent babysitters. Parents who live in must remember that the home belongs to the children. They are not to function as managers of the home, but as guests. They must allow their married children the freedom to rear their own children in accordance with their values. They must allow the married children the freedom to mature and succeed through their own mistakes and decisions. The "leaving" aspect of marriage can and should be a reality, even though the parents may live under the same roof. Attitudes, not locations, make the difference.

The situation can be a happy one, if the adults remember they are adults and live with Christ's Spirit within. A healthy attitude is to think of the situation as one family living together, rather than two families existing together. The parents should have the freedom to make suggestions without the fear of intruding.

The married children should have the liberty to include the parents in family plans without feeling burdened. The answer to any possible tension lies in adequate communication, with reciprocal respect and love.

Children

The Bible teaches that children are blessings to a family; however, we should not conclude that a childless couple is denied God's blessing. The interpersonal relationships between the parents and children help the parents to accept and live with their respective roles. These relationships also condition the developmental process of the children. Read Deuteronomy 7:13; Psalms 127:4, 5; 128:3, 4; Proverbs 10:1; 15:20; 17:6; 23:13-15).

Many people are too quick to blame the parents for the conduct of children. Although parents do share the responsibility for the life-style of the children, we must not forget that peer groups wield great power in molding children's attitudes. God commands children to obey their parents, partly because of the outside pressures on children. A child's attitude toward parents is included in the Ten Commandments, but the parents' attitude toward the children is not. This may be because of the recognized pull on the children by influences outside the home.

These varied magnetic pulls outside the home will inject disunity into the home, if they are heeded. Children are responsible to reject those pulls by adhering to the parents with honor and obedience. Children are to reject whatever goes against the teaching of their godly parents. That is the gist of the entire book of Proverbs. Read Proverbs 1:8-16, noting especially verses 8, 10, and 15: "Hear, my son, your father's instruction, and do not reject your mother's teaching" NASB.

During Old Testament times, failure on the part of

the children to heed their father's instruction was considered such a serious threat to the stability of the home and society that rebellious children were stoned to death (Deuteronomy 21:18-21). This sounds harsh, but outright rebellion that is not curbed can be taught from one generation to another (Jeremiah 28:16; 29:32) until a whole nation becomes rebellious (Isaiah 30:9; Ezekiel 2:3; 3:26, 27). We can see such results in our own nation, after an era of permissive behavior.

Children should be nurtured in the awareness of their responsibility to obey their parents. They will then be prepared for the powerful outside influences when they are old enough to be away from home seven hours a day in school. Children who make autonomous decisions must share part of the blame for a chaotic society.

Husband and Wife

Let us compare the relationship of the first husband and wife before they decided to sin with their relationship after they sinned. Many people feel that the relationship of the man and woman changed after their sin.

Adam and Eve's decision to sin was made before they had experienced any sin. The decision to sin is not reserved for the "fallen" state of humanity. They first sinned in the created state that God had declared was "very good" (Genesis 1:31). They had the capacity to choose evil as well as good. Man's desire for autonomy and independence, expressed in a rebellious decision, did not begin after the "fall," but before it. Otherwise, Satan would have had no one to tempt.

What was the woman's place before sin? The woman was a helper fit for the man. She was equal in dignity with man, created out of the same stuff as man. The two became one flesh. They were naked, but not ashamed. God never created the body as an evil prison house for the soul. The physical body is included in

God's declaration of "very good." What was woman's place after sin? She was still a helper fit for the man. She was still his complement, made by God to meet his needs. Sin did not diminish that status. Because she is needed as man's complement, the Old Testament honors her role: "Rejoice with the wife of thy youth" (Proverbs 5:18); "Whoso findeth a wife findeth a good thing, and obtaineth favour of the Lord" (18:22); "A prudent wife is from the Lord" (19:14); "Her price is far above rubies" (31:10).

Is the woman still equal in dignity? Yes! Are the husband and wife still considered a unit after the "fall"? Yes! Jesus always referred to the unit when asked about marriage. He never suggested that it was broken by sin. Do not miss the significance of this! We cannot permit male arrogance to continue. Arrogance is sin, no matter who expresses it. Because woman is from man (Genesis 2:21-25; 1 Corinthians 11:8), she shares something of man's character (1 Corinthians 11:7; "glory" means character). She becomes united with him in marriage (Genesis 2:24). The way a husband treats his wife is the way he treats himself (Ephesians 5:28). Competition was not to replace complementation after the fall into sin. Neither mate should try to exploit the other.

Were they still naked and not ashamed after the "fall"? No (Genesis 3:7, 10). Why? It certainly was not because their bodies were evil. God created those bodies with the obvious sexual differences. Was it because they had not engaged in sexual intercourse before sin? No. Sexual intercourse is not sin between married partners. To be naked is to be completely honest, with nothing hidden. Hiding is an act of deception, not of being honest or open. We humans are psychosomatically whole persons. When we have a reason to hide one aspect of our lives, we will often express that form of deception in other aspects also. I suspect that this is what happened in the Garden of

Eden. Before the fall, Adam and Eve had nothing to hide from each other or from God, so they did not deceive in any way. They were not ashamed of what they saw in each other. They were a unit. Adam was Eve's head, even before the fall, for her protection. As a unit they were to proceed in harmony toward life's goals. Then Eve began to hide some of her thoughts from Adam. She wanted to partake of the one tree that was forbidden, but she was not honest with her husband about it. She did not share her desires with her husband. This action created the weak spot that gave Satan leverage.

Anytime one begins to harbor thoughts that are out of harmony with the mutual goals of the unit, he needs to share those thoughts with his mate. Then direction and protection can be provided by the other mate. This is the interpersonal communication and confession husbands and wives need. But when one begins to harbor thoughts as a private matter, those thoughts can cut into the cleaving relationship of husband and wife. Satan will entice with those secret thoughts. Such enticements are calculated to draw the attention and commitment of one away from the other. Then the relationship between the two is no longer open and honest. When that happens, they can no longer stand to be naked. A cover-up takes place, and this may be expressed in either or both of two dimensions. The first is physical. One may not want to be seen naked by the other. We would probably be surprised how often this happens in marriage. There is not a complete openness between the two when this occurs. This is what happened between the first married partners: "I was naked; and I hid myself" (Genesis 3:10). This is not to condone or encourage the thoughts of some contemporaries who say we should have universal nakedness to foster universal honesty. Here we are discussing only husbands and wives. Genesis 2 and 3 concern only a husband and wife. Later, after the fall,

God provided clothing (3:21), and intended some clothing to be worn. He does expect a husband and wife to be naked in one another's presence without being ashamed.

The second dimension is a psychological cover-up. The tendency is for one to put on a psychological mask to prevent the other from discovering the wrong. Adam and Eve also experienced this dimension, for neither admitted his own desires. Instead, they both avoided personal responsibility for sin by placing the blame elsewhere (3:12, 13). Blaming others is a way of self-protection, a way of putting on a mask so others will not see the person as he really is. Adam and Eve were no longer living for the other's perfection but for their own protection. Each had erred, but neither wanted to be known as making a mistake, so each tried to cover up physically and psychologically.

If there is any one thing husbands and wives need to work out from the beginning of the marriage, it is to overcome the attitude of independence. Eve's initial mistake was in her act of individualism and independence from her husband, and then she sinned against God who ordained the unit of husband and wife. If each had functioned properly as part of the unit, drawing guidance, strength, and protection from the other, neither would have sinned. Harboring secret desires, hopes, and dreams serves to weaken the unit. Secretiveness unglues the cleaving relationship. Ideas and desires should be shared, discussed, and handled together, either condemning unhealthy desires and then being committed to live with that condemnation, or accepting those dreams and being mutually committed to make them come true.

Because husbands and wives live much of their day in separate environmental pressures, it is common for one mate to begin to harbor dreams and desires that the other does not have. The husband may associate with people who live with material goals and symbols.

The wife may have dreams based on the afternoon television serials that the husband never sees. Because of the diversity of daily activities, the husband and wife should keep their communication with each other open and grounded to their mutual goals.

Was the woman cursed after the fall to a position in life that was inferior to her position before the fall? No! Some persons believe that the fall took all rights away from the woman because she was cursed to the role of submission to her husband. In the Genesis account the wife's role with the husband and children did not change one bit after the fall.

Let us examine the passage that is usually considered. I have alphabetized the thoughts in this verse so that it will be easier to refer to them in the discussion that follows. "To the woman He said, [a] 'I will greatly multiply your pain in childbirth, in pain you shall bring forth children; [b] yet your desire shall be for your husband, [c] and he shall rule over you' " (3:16; NASB). The woman was not cursed, but afflicted. Only Satan was cursed (3:14). To say that God cursed the woman and the man is to misquote the Scripture. The above quotation includes a word about punishment, but also promise and protection.

The punishment is seen in statement (a): "I will greatly multiply your pain in childbirth." The literal translation of this is "By multiplying, I will multiply your sorrow indeed your pregnancy." This refers to the sorrow that accompanies the period of pregnancy. Why did God do this? I doubt that it was because God was angry and was repaying evil for evil. The multiplication in bodily sorrow was probably due to the imbalance in nature caused by man's separating from God. It is clear that man's sin brought disharmony into nature (Romans 8:19-23). Peace within nature is dependent upon man's being at peace with God. When one aspect of God's creation gets out of harmony with God, all other aspects of God's nature are affected, which is expressed in some degree of violence and pain. Thus, much of the "wrath of God" is built into the response of nature when it is out of harmony with God's original intention in creation. However, it is God's intention to restore harmonious relationships by reuniting all things, man and nature, in Christ (Ephesians 1:9, 10; Colossians 1:19, 20).

God's words to Adam and Eve were not curses, but announcements about the consequences caused by the imbalance in nature. Man's sin brought imbalance to God's created ecology. Eve's sin did not initiate pain in pregnancy and childbirth, but multiplied it. Now there would be a potential threat to the life of the mother. Pain, *per se*, is not evil. It is good. It is God's design for our protection, to alert us to danger. Nothing in Genesis suggests that Adam and Eve experienced no pain before the fall. If they had stubbed their toes on a rock, they would have felt pain. Pain is one of God's built-in protective devices. After the fall, nature posed a threat to life itself. Even the life-producing situation (pregnancy and childbirth) could now be a life-taking situation.

God would not permit the sorrow surrounding pregnancy to be so severe that the woman would not desire children. Jesus indicated the limited effect of this pain when He said, "A woman when she is in travail hath sorrow, because her hour is come: but as soon as she is delivered of the child, she remembereth no more the anguish, for joy that a man is born into the world" (John 16:21). Producing life will overshadow the presence of pain.

God promised that the presence of pain would not be so great that the woman would not desire further sexual intercourse with her husband. This is seen in statement (b): "Yet your desire shall be for your husband." The word "desire" refers to sexual intercourse (Song of Solomon 7:10). God's promise assures that the multiplication of pain in pregnancy and childbirth will not cut into the physical cleaving relationship of the husband and wife.

God further promised that the pain would not be so harsh that the woman would seek to live apart from the man. If the pain in the pregnancy would turn the woman against sexual intercourse, it would also lead to alienation from her husband. If that happened, she would not have her needs met as a person. God affirmed that this built-in result of sin would not interfere with the husband and wife roles. Statement (c), "And he shall rule over you," was part of God's promise, which was introduced by the word "yet" in (b). This word affirms that both sexual desire and the rule of the husband were present before the fall, and both would continue afterward. The sin of Adam and Eve did not disrupt the family unit or change the family roles.

Eve's place of submission was not given to her as part of God's curse (which He never gave), but as a part of God's creation. Adam was the head of the wife from the beginning. Part of Eve's sin was that she acted independently of her head in obeying the lure of the serpent. In that instance she acted as a self-appointed authority. Paul referred to this incident as a basis for refusing to let the woman teach or have authority over the man (1 Timothy 2:12-14). Some say that Paul was referring to the curse of the woman, but this is not so. He was referring to God's order of creation (v. 14). Why is it that a woman should not have authority over man? It disrupts the family order of God. Women's oppression over men was stated as one reason for the degeneration of Israel (Isaiah 3:12).

For Eve's own fulfillment and protection, not her inferiority, God promised that the man would continue to keep his place as head of the unit. We shall consider more specifically the roles of the partners, to see their value for individual growth and family harmony.

8

The Role of the Husband

People have overemphasized the wife's submission to her husband. Submissiveness is not the woman's exclusive responsibility, however. It is for any Christian, regardless of sex. Paul writes to the Christians at Ephesus, ". . . submitting yourselves one to another in the fear of God" (Ephesians 5:21). Then follows his grand section on husband and wife roles. Jesus also made the point clear in Matthew 20:25-27: " 'You know that the rulers of the Gentiles lord it over them, and *their great* men exercise authority over them. It is not so among you, but whoever wishes to become great among you shall be your servant, and whoever wishes to be first among you shall be your slave; just as the Son of Man did not come to be served, but to serve' " (NASB). No one can be a servant without submitting. It was Jesus' life-style (Matthew 20:28), and it is also to be the Christian's (Philippians 2:1-11). To be submitted to one another is a characteristic of being a Spirit-filled person (Ephesians 5:18-21).

What does submission mean? Not primarily blind obedience. The attitude of submission is summed up in the words of Paul: "Let each of us please his neighbor for his good, to his edification. For even Christ did not please Himself" (Romans 15:2, 3 NASB). The Greek word for submission carries the idea of a voluntary readiness of one person to renounce his own selfish will, desires, and rights for the sake of meeting the needs of another. It is the expression of *agape*-love. This is the characteristic of God (1 John 4:16), manifested in Jesus (John 1:14, 18; Colossians 1:15; Hebrews 1:3). Jesus was never blindly obedient to others, but He did serve them.

In this connotation the husband is to submit to the wife and the wife to the husband; that is, committed to live for the other's good, to meet each other's needs, to help the other reach fulfillment. This is what it means to edify another, to build him up toward his potential. Only as each lives for the other and responds to the life of the other can each become the mature person God intended.

Because the male and female are different, however, each mate has a different way to live for the other. The husband's submission is not expressed in the same way as the wife's. The male's basic need for fulfillment is to express, in companionship with his mate rather than competition with her, his basic characteristics of managing, penetrating, and mastering or leading. The woman's submission to his leadership enables the man to reach fulfillment.

The woman's submissive nature is expressed in tenderness, sympathy, care, peacemaking and dependency. The husband submits to his wife as he allows her basic nature to be fulfilled. He does this by being the kind of loving head of the unit that makes it easy for her to express her characteristics. He further lives to meet her need for protection as he functions as the kind of head she can respect and depend on. This is the kind of head Christ is to the church.

Head of the Family

The role of the husband is nowhere better described than in Ephesians 5:23-33; Colossians 3:19; 1 Timothy 3:1-6; 1 Peter 3:7. Headship of the husband involves a servant-kind of life with the wife. The man is head of the family by his service and sacrifice (Ephesians 5:25), his spiritual concern (vv. 26, 27), his love (v. 28). His headship is seen in his provision for the body (v. 29) and in his Christ-like character of gentleness (Colossians 3:19), thoughtfulness (1 Peter 3:7), patience, and lack of greed (1 Timothy 3:3). His overall management of the household includes hospitality and temperateness (1 Timothy 3:2), control over his children (v. 4), and giving instruction (Ephesians 6:4; 1 Timothy 3:2).

In my judgment, the qualifications of the elder in First Timothy refer first of all to the husband's style of life in the home. The second verse begins with the family, and the fourth ends with the family. I see no reason why the rest does not refer to his family life as well. Verse 5 would agree: "If a man does not know how to manage his own household, how will he take care of the church of God?" (NASB). The kind of disposition the husband and father has will indicate his disposition as an elder in the church. It is a serious mistake to elect an elder without knowing his life-style at home.

Real headship of the husband comes in the package of loveship (Ephesians 5:23, 25). For a man to live by this calls for real giving of self. It does not allow male chauvinism to dictate, but allows the Master's will and character to dominate. The wife's relationship to her husband is compared with Christ's relationship to the church. As the church is a responder to God's kind of love (1 John 4:10, 19), so the wife is a responder to her husband's kind of love. If the wife receives just *eros*-love (selfish), she will be motivated to return that kind to her husband. If she receives just *philos*-love, she will be prone to return that kind. If she receives *agape*-love, her needs will be met and she will be better able to return the same kind of love to him.

A man receives from his wife what he invests in her. When trouble arises, the husband should first of all examine what may be wrong with his own relationship with her. Above all, he should continue to love her. Christ loves the church no matter what weaknesses appear, and that is *agape*-love, which is called for in Ephesians 5:25: "Husbands, love your wives, even as Christ also loved the church, and gave himself up for it.'' With this kind of love a husband is to initiate the maintenance of the cleaving relationship. What a responsibility he has! It is he who sets the tempo for the whole family, and thus for all society. If his temperament is wrong, his wife's needs will not be fully met, and the children will be deficient as well. Thus, most of the blame for society's problems lies at the feet of the husbands, not the wives. God will hold the husband partly responsible for the character of his wife and children.

Headship like Christ's involves *the husband's humbly helping his wife*. Christ did not hesitate to give himself for the church. He did it in such humble ways as attending a wedding despite a busy schedule (John 2), missing meals (4), touching the despised sick (5), and giving up periods of rest (6:15-20). He did not retaliate when murmured against (7); He took the blunt of criticism, even though He was right (9). Jesus wept in front of a crowd (11), washed the feet of His disciples (13), and withstood mistreatment without rebuke (18—19:2). He died voluntarily so others could live (19:17, 18). This describes the kind of self-giving love that the husband is to have for his wife (Ephesians 5:25). Jesus determined to live that way from the start of His ''engagement'' to the church (Luke 4:18); so must the busband-to-be to his engaged.

Our teaching is backwards when we suggest that the home is the man's castle, to dominate as king. The home is not the husband's one-woman harem, to provide him with comforts and protect him from displeasure. The following scene is all too common today: The husband moves from the dinner table to occupy the television chair for the remainder of the evening, while the wife does the dishes, plays a bit with the children, helps with the homework, reads to them, helps them with the baths and preparation for bed, picks up the toys, and falls into bed literally exhausted. Then the husband cannot understand why she is too tired for sex. He has been excited through the television programs, but she has been exhausted from the tedious chores. Her lack of response may not indicate her lack of rapture late in the day so much as lack of respect earlier in the day.

Peter spoke about the kind of consideration the husband should have for his wife: "You husbands likewise, live with your wives in an understanding way, as with a weaker vessel, since she is a woman; and grant her honor as a fellow-heir of the grace of life, so that your prayers may not be hindered" (1 Peter 3:7; NASB). The words "grant her honor" mean to show respect. The effectiveness of a Christian man's prayers depends partly upon his fulfillment of his responsibility as head of the household.

Some husbands will say, "I'm not going to do that! It's not manly to show respect for my wife! I don't want to elevate *her*; I'm the head of the house!" Oh? Then you should read Philippians 2:3-7: "Do nothing from selfishness or empty conceit, but with humility of mind let each of you regard one another as more important than himself; do not merely look out for your own personal interests, but also for the interests of others. Have this attitude in yourselves which was also in Christ Jesus, who, although He existed in the form of God, did not regard equality with God a thing to be grasped, but emptied Himself, taking the form of a bond-servant" (NASB). Jesus demonstrated what it meant to be a man *par excellence*, and He was exalted through His humility (vv. 8, 9).

Headship also involves *putting self-interests in second place*. This means that neither the job, desire for advancement or prestige, leisure, hobbies, the dog, entertainment, nor sports should be allowed to come between the cleaving relationship with the wife. The husband must put ahead of his own interests his wife's well-being just as Christ puts our well-being first. Would you want Christ to value an automobile, sports, or the lodge above you? Remember, the bride is to be loved as Christ loves His bride, the church.

Headship involves *spiritual protection and care for the wife*. Christ gave himself up for His bride, for her spiritual well-being (Ephesians 5:25-27). "Even so [just like that] the husband should love his wife" (Ephesians 5:28). The husband must be the spiritual leader of his wife. How shameful it would be for a husband to lead his wife into Hell! The husband who is not a spiritual leader is not a man patterned after Christ.

Being the spiritual leader involves both attitudes and activities inside and outside the scheduled gatherings of the saints. The Bible teaches that the responsible spiritual leadership of the husband is more concerned with his activities and attitudes with his wife than with his activities and attitudes in the church meeting. For instance, effective prayers in the home depend upon the husband's gentlemanly attitude about his wife (1 Peter 3:7). Effective protection against the wife's yielding to sexual temptations depends upon the husband's fulfilling his duty to his wife sexually (1 Corinthians 7:3). The stability of the family depends upon the husband's manifesting the attitudes of a spiritual leader at home (1 Timothy 3:2-5). Certainly the involvement in the church meeting is not to be neglected, but it cannot replace a man's responsibility at home.

Headship involves *affectionate care*. A husband is not only to love his wife as Christ loves the church, but to nourish and cherish her as he does his own body (Ephesians 5:28, 29). As the church is now the body of Christ, the woman is the body of man. Whatever a man does to the church he does to Christ, and whatever he does to his wife he does to himself.

"Nourish" and "cherish" were words used to describe a nurse's motherly and tender care for a child. As a child needs more than mere physical necessities, so does the wife. A healthy child needs a soft hand and sweet talk, and so does the wife. She thrives on the hand-holding and I love you's, far more than the man does. If you want to put your wife on cloud nine, just reach down and clasp her hand as you walk down the street, or wink at her across the table in a restaurant. Maybe the married man gets little thrill out of that, but he is made differently. The woman needs those tender expressions of the man's love.

Too often we have turned around whose initial responsibility it is to nourish and cherish. Many men act like boys wanting "mother" to feed them so they can go and play their "games" and then be comforted when they get hurt. Biblically, the husband has that initial role. Have you ever noticed how little girls need Daddy's lap and his hugs? These little girls are mothers-in-the-making. When they become mothers, they still need such affectionate attention. When they receive it they will respond with nourishing and cherishing of the husband, not out of duty but out of delight.

Someone may ask, "What if the wife doesn't respond with the kind of love the husband gives? What if she continues to nag, nettle, and nip?" Here again, the husband has the responsibility to love as Christ loves. He loves regardless of the response. His love is steadfast. His love for the church is not altered by the church's negative response. Neither should the husband's love be altered by the wife's negative reaction. He has the responsibility to continuously initiate love, whatever the circumstances. This is a tall order, but that is what it means to love the bride as Christ loves His bride.

The price may be high, but the dividends are fantastic. Unloveliness can change to loveliness. As Christ's kindness is the power to change the church (Romans 2:4), so the husband can change his wife. Indeed, he has the responsibility to so love her that he may present her to God as changed, sanctified, cleansed, and holy. It is in the context of making this point that Paul wrote, "For this cause shall a man leave his father and mother, and shall be joined unto his wife, and they two shall be one flesh" (Ephesians 5:31). May each husband love his wife as himself, for she is a part of him.

Let us now consider what being the head of the family unit does not mean. *Headship does not mean superiority*. From the creation, male and female were to share equality in dignity, though diversity in function. There are psychological, physical differences, and functional differences, but there are no differences in status. Man is no more superior to woman because he is her head than God is superior to Jesus because He is Jesus' head. The New Testament teaches that God is Christ's head (1 Corinthians 11:3), but it also affirms their essential equality (John 1:1; 10:30; Philippians 2:6; 1 John 5:20).

The chain of command for the family is not pictured as a vertical chart with man at the top, followed by woman, then children. The picture is more like a circular chart, with God in the center and the family members rotating around Him. God is nowhere *between* the members, but remains in the center of the family unit. The circular chart affirms that man is the head, but also recognizes that each partner has a need for the other and complements the other. No one is "put down." The true picture on a vertical chart should show the man at the bottom, since lordship comes from serving all (Matthew 20:25-28). It would show service and support (bottom to top), not dictatorship (top to bottom).

Headship does not mean lawgiving. The husband is not a lawgiver such as a drill sergeant or four-star general. Being the head of the family does not mean that the father makes all decisions in isolation from or without consideration of the desires of the wife and children. The family relationship is to be one of fellowship, *koinonia*-style (Philippians 2:2). That is a common oneness with a common-mindedness.

The wife has some abilities that the husband does not have. There are areas in which women are more knowledgeable than men. It would be in opposition to why God created the woman, if husbands did not appreciate their wives' abilities or disregarded them. The husband's decisions must not thwart the charisma (gift) God has given the wife. They must not prevent her from being a complement to him. The Bible affirms that a woman opens her mouth with wisdom (Proverbs 31:26), and a man should incline his ear to the words of the wise (22:17; 1:8; 6:20-23). One is a fool who does not. This does not mean, however, that the wife should assume authority over the man.

Although the husband will not make all the decisions without discussions with his wife, he will be held responsible for all the decisions made. The wife will not be held responsible for the bad decisions her husband has made, but she will be held responsible in regard to submitting to him. If there is a disagreement about which decision should be made, the husband should decide and the wife should abide by it. The husband should not take advantage of this, however. If he realizes he has made a bad decision, he should be mature enough to admit it. There is no need to multiply the error by deciding not to affirm or alter a mistake.

Headship does not mean patronizing. The wife is not to be treated as an inadequate child. As Christ has confidence in the church, so should the husband have confidence in his wife. Christ delegated authority and responsibility to the church. He guides and equips the church to carry out His plan and wishes. The church makes decisions in keeping with these. The husband and wife should act in like manner. That is the kind of functioning fellowship we see in the Godhead, even though the Father is recognized as head. For instance,

God, Jesus, and the Holy Spirit can all be referred to as Creator in the Bible. Both God and Jesus are called Savior. All three are called sources of peace. What one does, they all do. In the same way, the husband and wife must work as a team with mutual consent that the husband is the human captain of this team. A family without a functioning head is in as much trouble as a physical body without a functioning head. This does not mean that the head is superior, for all the parts are needed (see 1 Corinthians 12:14 ff.). But a family with two heads is as much a freak as a body with two heads.

For the sake of order, God has established headship in the family. Any organization needs a head, which is not to say that the one appointed is necessarily the most intelligent. A vice-president of a company may be more brilliant than the president, and must be in some areas in order to be a good complement. The two should not compete for decision-making successes, but cooperate in mutual trust and confidence. They need to share each other's abilities, resources, and experiences. When a decision cannot be made by mutual consent, the vice-president must concede to the president's decision and abide by it. This system works the same way in the family.

The husband must trust his wife and make her feel comfortable making decisions in delegated areas. Just as the church has many rights (order of worship, time, frequency of meetings), so does the wife. Her rights are all under the umbrella of living in unity with her husband. When the husband functions as a loving head without wishy-washy attitudes, he meets the wife's need to depend on someone. She can trust him as she leans upon him, because he is living out the male role as God intended. She is actually freer to function with her God-given nature. With a husband who functions as he should, she does not have to drain her energies trying to think and live like a technological man. If the husband is a loving head, the wife is free to express her basic nature of sympathy, care, kindness, tenderness, and nurture to him. If the husband thwarts her expression of these qualities at home by forcing her to live like a man (making male decisions), her femininity will be imprisoned. In a recent survey, one thousand wives were asked what they needed most from their husbands. All replied, "his authority."

As the husband must be head of the wife, so Christ must be the head of the husband. The husband must respond to Christ's headship in such a way that his decisions will be Christ's. The husband has no right to make decisions without regard to his Head. He is not to live in competition with his Head in decision-making. If his decisions would differ from Christ's, he must shelve them and abide by Christ's. The husband must say to Christ what Christ said to God, "Not my will, but thine, be done." Christ follows God's will. The husband follows Christ's will. The wife follows the husband's will. The children follow the parents' will. Thus the family will be Christian in function as well as in name.

9

The Role of the Wife

No one has stated the role of the wife better than God himself: "I will make him a helper suitable for him" (Genesis 2:18; NASB). She is man's special companion and complement. Being a helper fit for the man involves her submission to him. The Christian wife is to submit to her husband with the same attitudes that undergird her submission to the Lord (Ephesians 5:22). The kind of results she receives from submitting to the Lord, blessing and fulfillment, she receives from submitting to her husband. In fact, a wife who does not submit to her husband is not submitting to the Lord. God designed that woman should submit to her husband. To fail to do so is to rebel against God's order for the family.

It would be easy to speak of the wife's submission as being a mark of her stupidity. Yet submission elsewhere in God's design never marks stupidity. It was not stupid for Jesus to submit to His Father. Can you imagine what would have happened if Jesus refused to submit to God? Coherence would have given way to chaos. Life would have given way to death. To refuse to submit is not a mark of maturity or wisdom, but of arrogance. It is not stupid for the physical body to submit to the body's head. As the body's coordination is beautiful as it submits to its head, so the marriage is beautiful as the wife submits to her head.

It would also be easy to see submission as suppression of the woman's individuality. Yet the man is woman's counterpart and complement as designed by God, just as she is his. Woman reaches maturity and is free to function with all the potentialities of her femininity through her submission to him. Too often the wife's submission is seen as impersonal; that is, without regard for her uniqueness as an individual.

God's intention in making the woman was that she would contribute to his life with her uniqueness: one life created by God united with another life created by God. Each woman has her own individuality, her own charisma. To submit to her husband in the highest sense is not to bypass that uniqueness, or to suppress it, but to allow it to develop so that what the woman is as a person will be shared with her husband. God wants expressive or creative submission, not computerized submission. Each woman has a self to share.

We must never equate a submissive wife with a suppressed wife. Legalism will do that, but love will not. The husband is given the mandate to love his wife as Christ loved the church. Loving the church, Christ freed it to function according to its intended nature (Galatians 5:1).

In expressing her ideas, projects, abilities, and personality for the well-being of her husband, the wife must remember to pour her femininity into those expressions. Many women seem to object to being women and try to think and act like men. Neither husband, home, nor society needs that. Most important of all, the woman does not need that. When she does this, the balance of maleness and femaleness is lost, and something of the image of God is blurred. God's image is expressed through the combination of maleness and femaleness, not through either one alone (see Genesis 1:27, 28, where ''man'' refers to both male and female).

The husband must allow the wife to develop and express her potentialities as a person, and to see these as a complement to him rather than competition or a threat. Our society is worsened when a women's individuality is suppressed in her submission. We can only guess how much better our world could be if women's creativity were shared in many areas of life. We can no longer use the Bible as our reason for preventing half of humankind from participating in planning and decision-making. The good woman in Proverbs 31:10-31 expressed her individuality, interests, and abilities in many ways. In this passage of Scripture is the grandest word portrait ever painted by a pen: "Who can find a virtuous woman? for her price is far above rubies."

Here woman's inestimable value is introduced. This evaluation challenges male chauvinism. The rest of the chapter gives the reasons for the statement of her value.

"Her husband doth safely trust in her" (v. 11). She is trustworthy. He has full confidence in her handling of the affairs that accompany managing a household. She can be trusted with the total bank account. How can this be? Because she and her husband are a unit. Neither person is free from the influence of the other when they are separated, for to be "one flesh" means they are committed to the same goals and to function as a team in achieving those goals. If the husband does not love his wife, and if the wife does not submit to her husband, this kind of trust cannot develop.

"She will do him good and not evil all the days of her life" (v. 12). The rest of the chapter rotates around this verse. She lives for his fulfillment. That is *agape*-love and the result of submission. In her submission to his headship, she provides the home environment the man needs to live òut his basic male nature. Many men cannot express that maleness at work, because they are under the authority of others. At home a man needs an encourager and supporter. God has provided it in the nature of a woman. When the wife does not function as a submissive woman, she brings her husband evil in the form of his lack of fulfillment.

"She seeketh wool, and flax, and worketh willingly with her hands" (v. 13). Her disposition for caring is

expressed in providing for her family. She is industrious and enjoys it. How can she be delighted with such a life? Because her husband is not forcing her to act like a man by his failure to function in his own God-designed role.

"She is like the merchants' ships; she bringeth her food from afar" (v. 14). As ships sail away to bring goods from afar, so she will travel to bring home the bargains. Doesn't that sound like a woman today, driving twenty miles to take in a sale?

"She riseth also while it is yet night, and giveth meat to her household, and a portion to her maidens" (v. 15). Her family never leaves the house in the morning without breakfast. In that day, the woman would rise many hours before daylight in expressing her concern for the family's needs and welfare. Some arose just after midnight. Women did not have biscuits in a can, cake mixes, or frozen pies. They did their baking daily. You say, "I could do that too, if I had maidens as she had!" Most women in the United States do have maidens: the automatic washer and dryer, furnace with thermostat, electric iron, water heater, refrigerator, sweeper, automatic dishwasher, and garbage disposal. These maidens don't talk back! These can be considered as one of the provisions of God to free the woman to use her creativity in more interpersonal activities. She has more time to pour her selfhood into the lives of her family and into the future of the community. May she do so in complementation to the male contribution and not in competition with it.

"She considereth a field, and buyeth it" (v. 16). I can just hear the men asking, "Where did she get that kind of money?" She saved it from her earnings. Evidently she saw a bargain in a field and decided it would save the family in the long run if they could raise their own food and not have to travel "as a ship" to gather it. The field would allow her more time to be near her family. Not only did she buy that field, but she

planted it herself. The considerate woman today does the same kind of thinking where the interests of her family are involved.

"She girdeth her loins with strength, and strengtheneth her arms" (v. 17). She is not weak or lazy, but more is involved here than strength for her housekeeping tasks. If she is the right kind of encourager and supporter of her husband and family, she needs a unique kind of strength. It is this strength that enables her to keep the household on an even keel in times of crises or disharmony.

"She maketh herself coverings of tapestry; her clothing is silk and purple" (v. 22). Even though she is busy working for her family, she does not neglect herself. She loves to dress like a woman and sets a standard of womanliness for her daughters. By observing her they learn how womanhood is expressed and fulfilled.

"Her husband is known at the gates" (v. 23). Her husband is free to function as a man because the wife is functioning as a woman. He does his part in business and civic affairs at the gates of the city, confident that the home is well tended. He is able to make his contribution and become prominent because his wife is a real complement for him. He rises to the place of "elder," partly because she has lifted him by her wifely support.

This does not mean that he is in the public eye all day while she stays home. She is merchandizing: *"She maketh fine linen, and selleth it; and delivereth girdles unto the merchant"* (v. 24). The thesis that a woman is never to work outside the home cannot be supported by Scripture. Here is the wife of a prominent city official working outside the home. She dabbled in real estate, manufactured products, and sold them. Her work did not interfere with her family responsibilities, however. Neither did she work outside the home because she rebelled against her role as wife and mother.

No doubt the quality of her work was in part related to her joy as a wife and mother.

"She openeth her mouth with wisdom; and in her tongue is the law of kindness" (v. 26). She is not the type who is seen but not heard. Her speech is not stupid or sarcastic. She is a well-balanced woman, secure in her role. She has dignity, and evidently she enjoys being a woman. She does not have to use her intellectual abilities to "lord" it over others. She combines wisdom and kindness.

"She looketh well to the ways of her household" (v. 27). She is not too "intelligent" for humdrum duties. Through the medium of her household duties her wisdom has the most opportunity to be expressed. Because she functions as a mature, well-balanced, and happy woman, her family blesses and praises her. She is accepted and loved. Her children have no desire to run away from her, and her husband has no reason to "cut her down." This is a picture of a happy, balanced family. The leaving of parents, the cleaving relationship, and the oneness are all evident.

This woman in Proverbs has reached the height of meaningfulness because she respects the Lord's will for her life (v. 30). This is her liberation. She is "praised in the gates," and who is praising her there? Her own husband, the one person who means the most to her and to whom she means the most. He is her number-one fan! If more men would respect their wives and praise them, especially before others, more children would learn respect for womanhood. Children need that lesson badly. If fathers would teach respect for women by their own example, we would see fewer girls mistreated, fewer prostitutes, fewer unwed mothers, and fewer belittled wives. Of course, the wife must do her part to deserve the respect.

Since the husband has a basic need to be a decision-maker, the woman helps fulfill that need by respecting and submitting to it. Wives must ask, "Am

I making it easy for my husband to be the leader?''
One of the major hindrances of leadership is fear of
failure. That fear is intensified if harsh criticism is received when wrong decisions have been made. The
more a wife criticizes the husband's decisions or is
upset with his mistakes, the more the husband will
relinquish his leadership to her. The more the wife
becomes the leader, the more she will disrespect her
husband. The husband may not have grown up in a
home where the man was the leader. If so, time and
patient encouragement will be necessary for him to
learn how to fulfill the responsibility of leadership in
his new family. If the wife takes away the headship
from her husband, she is violating the God-ordained
order for the home. The wife's attitude and reaction to
the husband's decisions should help him to accept his
leadership responsibility.

Children must be able to recognize the male-female
roles in the home. To blur them is to create an identity
crisis. Boys need to see in the father what it means to
be a fulfilled man, and girls need to see in the mother
what it means to be a fulfilled woman. Each child
needs to grow up realizing and accepting his or her
own sex identity and role. The blurring of the sex roles
(men living like submissive women, and women living
like domineering men) has been directly related to
homosexuality, rape, and transexual operations.

Fathers and mothers must accept themselves first.
By doing so they will help to fulfill each other's sex
role in the family. For instance, wives should not expect the men to be ''mothers.'' Man's basic makeup is
not fulfilled by habitually changing diapers, cooking,
doing dishes, or cleaning the house. There is certainly
nothing wrong with the husband's helping with these
chores in needed times, but a whole life-style of play-
ing the wife's role will not be satisfying to him.
Mothers should not have their sons do the dishes on a
regular basis, nor should fathers have the daughters

drive tractors on a regular basis. Give each child the chores that suit his or her sexual identity.

The wife's submission to her husband is not just to help fulfill his need by allowing his basic characteristics to be expressed. Her submission also serves to fulfill her needs in three areas of protection: (1) Physically the woman is the weaker sex and is vulnerable to attack. She is secure as she knows she can submit to her husband's care. (2) Emotionally, the woman becomes upset more easily than a man over trivial matters. She has a tendency to take everything personally. When another family is having troubles, she can be sympathetic, imagine all sorts of things, and worry. This causes emotional stress. She can spare herself and her family as she submits to her husband's reactions and to his decision about how to help the troubled family. (3) Spiritually, Satan will try to use her, or trick her. Satan discovered from the garden experience that the easiest way to get to the man is through the woman. Women must be aware of this trick of Satan. Her protection from this deception is to submit to her husband's will. She should make the kind of decisions when away from him that she would make in his presence. Her husband's authority is her protective shield, which actually frees her to live with more femininity. Thus she submits to him the frustrations and anxieties that the man can cope with more easily. The more she allows him to have the authority and responsibility, the more her own needs will be met. If the wife does not do this, she is committing marital suicide.

What is the limit of submission? Ephesians 5:24 answers this: "As the church is subject unto Christ, so let wives be to their own husbands in every thing." A better translation would be "in every way or situation." In every situation, the wife should live for her husband's good. It would not be for his good for her to submit to an act of immorality or willful disobedience to God. We have a classic example of this in Acts 5. Ananias decided to lie to God; his wife decided to submit to his decision. Peter did not commend Sapphira for submitting to her husband in that act, but rebuked her. A wife must not submit in those situations which violate her obligations to God, but one must be careful and sure about what those obligations are.

Peter said that Christian wives may win unbelieving husbands by their quiet and gentle spirit "which in God's sight is very precious" (1 Peter 3:1-16). If her life-style is Christ's, a woman can win her husband without a word. This means that she doesn't nag him about becoming a Christian. She doesn't slip tracts in his lunch box, glue Scripture verses to his shaving mirror, or read the Bible aloud to him. She lives a serving role that recognizes his headship. By fulfilling her obligation to God, by being the best Christian servant and witness she can be, she will become her best self. The husband will then see that all this is in his own best interest. Her life will demonstrate the kind of behavior that will attract him to the Savior she loves.

No wonder the older women are to teach and train the younger women to "love their husbands, to love their children, to be discreet, chaste, keepers at home, good, obedient to their own husbands, that the word of God be not blasphemed" (Titus 2:3-5). Do we use the older women in the church for this task? We should. We aren't restoring New Testament Christianity until we do. Is it possible that failure to use the older women in that way contributes to the family upsets, trials, and other messes within the church? If one generation of women is not taught concerning unity in the home, there will be no unity in the home, and thus none in the church.

10

A Word to Parents

Children are blessings from God to a family, but in earlier periods of history children have been given second-rate citizenship. Just before Jesus came to earth, children were not considered significant. Roman law permitted the father to sell or kill his children. When a new baby was brought to the father and he named it, the child lived; if he turned and walked away, the baby was abandoned.

Within that kind of atmosphere, Paul wrote a revolutionary word of advice: "Fathers, provoke not your children to wrath: but bring them up in the nurture and admonition of the Lord" (Ephesians 6:4). Parents are God-ordained custodians of their children. What the children become depends largely upon the parents' relationship with them.

Our children are becomers, adults in the making. Whatever happens during their development affects the kind of adults they will become. For instance, during infancy a child needs to develop a sense of trust in others. That trust is achieved primarily through the quality of the care the mother gives the baby. If this early need is not met, the child will find it difficult to trust people when he is older. How a child's basic needs are met through his interpersonal relationships with people will form attitudes and frames of reference that will make up the child's adolescent personality.

Some experts on child development advocate that parents know what children need at each crisis stage in their lives. This is too idealistic, however. Few parents can function as knowledgeable child psychologists, nor is that desirable! Then how can parents meet the needs of children at these crucial times? Eric Erikson, an expert on the subject, and author of *Identity Youth and Crises*, advises that the healthy child be given a reasonable amount of proper guidance. The child can then be trusted to obey the inner laws of development. It follows that he will become a properly balanced adult. This raises the question: What constitutes "a reasonable amount of proper guidance"? How much reading of books about current theories of child-rearing is necessary for a parent? The late Andras Angyal, an expert in understanding personality, gives some of the best advice in his book, *Neurosis and Treatment*. He wrote that the understanding needed for a child's emotional growth does not depend so much on information as on the parents' attitude and the right kind of love.

Rearing children properly, then, rests largely upon quality love. What is the content of "quality love"? Let us turn to the Bible. We believe that God gave His Word to us partly to share with us the correct content of love. That is why Paul admonishes us to bring up our children in the discipline and instruction of the Lord. When we follow God's Word, we follow His way of love (John 15:7, 10; 1 John 4:12, 16). To be assured that what we are doing for our children is an expression of real love is to follow God's advice, since He is the source of love (1 John 4:7, 16). Rearing children according to God's advice assures us that those children will become quality adults. In fact, God promises precisely that when He said, "Train up a child in the way he should go [our responsibility], and when he is old, he will not depart from it [God's promise, based on the fulfillment of our responsibility]" (Proverbs 22:6).

"Train up" comes from a Hebrew word originally used to describe what a midwife did when she rubbed a solution on the roof of a baby's mouth to induce an interest in sucking. Later the term came to refer to dedicating a person or thing; then it came to mean "education." In Proverbs, the context refers to educating a person to dedicate himself to accept God's life-style for his own life-style. We cannot force a person to do this, but we can bring him up in a way that creates in him an interest to accept God's way of life for himself. While it is true that one cannot make a horse drink water after leading him to it, he can put salt in his food to make him thirsty. It is the same with rearing children. How much salt are you putting into your children's lives to create a thirst within them to adopt God's life-style for themselves?

"In the way he should go" has a two-fold application:

First, there is a specific application for each child. In early times, rabbis stressed this application. Each child has his own abilities, interests, aptitudes, and capabilities. Thus to train up a child in the way *he* should go would mean that the parents should train him to develop his own personality and capabilities. We must know the abilities of each child in order to help his individuality to emerge. We must not try to pour our child into the mold of the neighbor's child or the child we wish we could have been.

Second, there is a general application, for there is a *way* that everyone should go, regardless of his uniqueness. It is the way of living out the image of God in moral living. We are to teach morality in our homes, and this is often misunderstood. It can never be lived in isolation from others. Morality or immorality is expressed most of all through interpersonal relationships. Training up a child in the way he should go means educating him to live with proper interpersonal relationships. Most of the book of Proverbs deals with this subject. There we read about submission, righteousness, justice, equality, loyalty, integrity, faithfulness, humility, and steadfastness. We seem to have read "for adults only" into these characteristics, while every personal attitude and activity that is prominent in the life of an adult was conditioned during his formative years. We must therefore consider how God's intention for conduct is being taught to our children. How can some of God's eternal principles for life become a part of child training?

The book of Proverbs provides us the best source for these principles. Space allows for the discussion of only a few to show how they relate to child training. The reader may continue to study the book, find more principles, and apply them to child training. As we parents seek to transmit these principles to our children, we are both loving them and teaching them how to love others. We are also laying the best foundation for preventing the development of serious personality conflicts later.

"He that covereth a transgression seeketh love; but he that repeateth a matter separateth very friends" (17:9). No age group is exempted from the application of this principle. Anyone who tattles will alienate friends. Children experience this early in life. If tattling is not curbed, they will grow up distrusting one another. That is one reason some brothers and sisters grow apart in their teens. Their lack of trust has hampered their friendship. If tattling is not arrested early, it may later emerge in the form of adult gossiping. I suspect we would have less slander in the church if we had less backbiting at home.

"A soft answer turneth away wrath: but grievous words stir up anger" (15:1). This also applies to all age groups. The application of this principle not only helps to maintain peace in the home, but also teaches a child not to react to people in the same way they act toward him. This is a vital lesson to transmit through child training, for it teaches children not to retaliate. When children can learn that lesson by observing interpersonal relationships at home, they are well on the way toward developing mature personalities. The New Testament admonition to refrain from returning evil

86

for evil but to give a blessing instead (1 Peter 3:9) begins with the application of this Proverb. Many of the problems within a church (especially on a church board) could have been avoided were this admonition a part of the life-style of the adults.

The way we speak with one another at home affects not only the mental but also the physical well-being of each other. Alienation is a major cause of physical disease (dis-ease). The use of our tongues can bring about actual physical harm or healing to someone else (Proverbs 12:18; 16:24; 18:21). There is a correlation between parents who yell and scream at each other and their children who are sick much of the time. The medical profession affirms that much physical disease is caused by lack of interpersonal fellowship. A surgeon lectured on the topic, "A Physical Fitness Program for Christians," which I thought would be a speech about exercises. Instead he used Proverbs 12:18 as a text: "There is that speaketh like the piercings of a sword: but the tongue of the wise is health." He outlined the importance of following this for the health of people. He said we could reduce medical bills by fifty percent, if we followed God's will in interpersonal life. No wonder Paul tells us to use our speech only for building up (Ephesians 4:29), and James says that the man who does not offend in word is perfect (mature) (3:2).

"It is not good to have respect of persons in judgment" (Proverbs 24:23). We are doing harm to a child when we blame others for his lack of achievement. For instance, rather than admit that another child's entry at the 4-H fair is better than our child's entry, we may either blame the judge or criticize the other entry. To our child this can become an early lesson not to accept the consequences for his actions, not to trust the honest appraisal of others, and not to respect the achievements of others. Such poor judgment prevents our children from learning to accept

failure, and at the same time teaches them to rationalize as a way out of difficulty.

"Treasures of wickedness profit nothing" (10:2). This refers to advantages or goods obtained by illegal or underhanded means. Children can either learn or not learn this very early through our reaction to their cheating in games or lessons. If we laugh at their cheating episodes, we are teaching them that such means are acceptable and advantageous. How they learn to play games may later be reflected in their undertakings as adults. Cheating can help foster a lifestyle of selfishness and introvertism.

"Labour not to be rich" (23:4). This principle does not depreciate wealth, but rather advises one against making its acquisition the chief aim of his industry. Children develop their reasons for working from their parents' philosophy about working, but also from the ways we parents motivate them to do their chores. Do they hear us complain about our jobs and realize we remain at them only for the pay? Do we bribe them to do their work? Why do we approve or disapprove their choice of careers? What do they learn from us about being careful, thorough, and conscientious on the job?

One of society's desperate needs is for workers who take pride in the contribution their job makes toward their fellowmen. We need people on the assembly line who will do their best because a fellow human will be using the product. We need this philosophy, not only on the assembly line, but also in the administrative offices. Usually philosophy about work flows from the top down; therefore, administrators cannot expect their workers to be really concerned about the finished product, if they sense that the company is concerned only about profit.

Many people live a lifetime without feeling they have contributed to the well-being of others. What a tragic waste! What a difference the right philosophy of work would make, not only to the self-satisfaction of employers and employees, but also to the trust people would have in the products they purchase, even to the economy itself. Inflation could be reduced considerably if manufacturers did not have to build into the prices of their merchandise a high percentage of recalls and repairs under guarantee. What are company and union people doing to help develop a correct philosophy of work among us? What are parents doing?

Working for pay does not produce the satisfaction that working for people does. It is one thing to work for pay, but another to get paid for working. When we work just for pay, our work is mundane and often inferior, for our goal is reached every payday.

Our family recently bought a new house built by men who worked for pay, without pride in the contribution their workmanship could make to the family who would live in the house. They were concerned only about getting the job done so that another house could be started. The end product shows it. What a waste of workmanship! What a loss in a contribution to a neighborhood and the comfortableness of families to come. I strongly suspect that most of these workmen learned in childhood this philosophy toward work. We need to teach our children about values. We can begin when they are little by letting them see what contribution their little chores make toward the well-being of the family.

Children usually enjoy working with parents, but too often we are prone to say, "You're too young." When my son was four years old, he wanted to help me wash the car and change the oil. I let him, and he has never stopped enjoying doing that. I hope he never stops enjoying it. He is now seven and wants to help me mow the grass. I let him, and keep telling him how much fun it is and how by keeping the lawn mowed we are helping to keep God's earth beautiful. I hope that when he is a teenager he will still enjoy it and see the contribution of doing it. Even our little daughter has the same philosophy about work. Where did she learn it? From him. She delights in helping her mother do the dishes, set the table, and bake cookies. If we do not teach and encourage children to fill some of their time with responsibilities, they will not know how to handle leisure time when they are older. Meaningless time breeds mean trouble in the land.

"He that covereth his sins shall not prosper: but whoso confesseth and forsaketh them shall have mercy" (28:13). Are we helping our children follow this principle by having a home environment that helps them to be honest when they err? Do they experience our love regardless of their mistakes? If that is their concept of acceptation (I love you if—), they may become adults who live only for acceptance of others. This could inhibit their ability to expose their real selves when they become adults. They may become shackled to the expectations of others and thus never develop their uniqueness.

Children need parents in whom to confide when they really "blow it." If they do not, they will be uncomfortable in their parents' presence when they have done wrong. They may adopt many kinds of defense mechanisms to prevent communication with their parents. Failure to feel accepted by the closest family members when one has "goofed" may affect his ability to be honest with his mate when he marries. The parable of the prodigal son reveals what can happen when a child knows he can be honest with his parents.

"Correct thy son, and he shall give thee rest; yea, he shall give delight unto thy soul" (29:17). God approves of spanking as an expression of love (13:24), "Dear Abby" notwithstanding. Children realize that discipline is a way that parents show their concern for children's behavior. A parent once said that her daughter remarked, "I'd hate to be Jane." When

asked why she replied, "She has never had a spanking. Her folks don't love her." Elementary teachers can easily spot the pupils who receive no discipline at home. Those children will do mischievous things just to receive the discipline that reassures them someone does care about them. The progressive philosophy of child training (let the child decide for himself) has failed. Even some of its chief proponents have renounced it. God had told us long ago that training a child demanded adult decisions rather than children's desires (22:6). A parent who does not discipline his child has set his heart upon the destruction of the child's personality (19:18). Children need parental guidance most when they want it the least.

Sometimes I think we love cherries more than children, for we will drive stakes beside young cherry tree sprouts to give them direction in growth. Yet we are afraid we are interfering if we dictate standards for the direction of our children. Discipline is necessary, but though discipline with the rod is sometimes necessary, this is not to be the first and only kind of discipline to administer. Children need various kinds, depending upon the situation. One of the worst things a parent can do, however, is to promise a spanking and then not give it. That is being dishonest with the child. It makes him wonder what you really do mean and how you want him to act. This is one reason why many children lose respect for their parents. Parents should always fulfill their promises so that the children will always believe them. Many children have learned that parents do not mean what they say unless their voices are raised in anger. How familiar is this scene:

Mother says, "It's time to pick up your toys, honey."

Janie thinks, *I've got five more minutes. She is in a good mood.*

Mother says, more firmly, "Janie, please get your toys together."

Janie thinks, *I still have time.*

Mother asks, "Janie, are you picking up the toys?"

Janie thinks, *Playtime is about over.*

Mother says, loudly this time, "Janie, get those toys picked up!"

Janie thinks, *I can spin this top one last time.*

Mother, with an angry voice accompanied by heavy footsteps, "Janie, get busy!"

Janie begins picking up the toys.

Janie needs to know what Mother means when she says "honey" in her calm, friendly voice. Janie will never know that, as long as Mother does not follow through with discipline that first friendly, unheeded request.

Any discipline must be coupled with an explanation and followed up with acceptance. It is a good practice to say, "I am punishing you for—, because I love you." The discipline itself should be executed in love, not anger. Discipline is to be done for a child's restraint and guidance, not for revenge and self-gratification of the parents.

There will be times when parents will make mistakes in discipline. We may discover that a child did not do the wrong we thought he did. When that happens, we must always admit our error, apologize, and ask for forgiveness. Recently, I pressed our five-year-old daughter into admitting a wrong I thought she had done, then I spanked her. Afterward I discovered she had not been guilty. After asking for her forgiveness, I pondered the question of why she had admitted doing something she had not done. Then it hit me! She had sensed that I did not believe her when she denied her guilt, so, to fulfill *my* wishes she admitted it. If a five-year-old will react like that when she feels she is not trusted, how would a teenager react if he feels his parents do not trust him? He will reason, "I might as well go ahead and do this wrong that my parents think I am doing. They won't believe me anyway." Children will try to live up to the trust or image we have of them. Let's give them something high to reach for!

At the same time, children will not be motivated to live up to your image of them if they do not respect you. Their respect for parents will be highest when the parents are living a sincere life of unselfish love. Their honest relationship with each other and with the children will determine the response. Respect can never be acquired by lavishing a person with things, but it will be acquired by living the principles of truth.

Satan knows several things about the significance of the parent-child relationship:

Parents are God-ordained custodians of the young. The best way to get children out of touch with God is to distract the parents from their primary responsibility as guardians.

The child's development depends largely upon the parents' decisions. Satan will try to interfere with their unity of agreement.

The best time to fill people's hearts with folly is when they are young.

A team of at least three is necessary to rear a child properly: mother, father, and God. Satan will try his best to break up this team.

Bible teaching is the best curriculum for child training. Satan will seek to keep us too busy to share Scriptural truths with our children, lest we will produce a generation of Timothys who are completely equipped for lives of righteousness (2 Timothy 3:14-17).

It is hoped that parents reading this book will make an effort to know the Word of God and to teach the truths in the Bible, "when you sit in your house, when you walk about, when you lie down, and when you rise up." (Deuteronomy 6:7). Teach the Bible, so that your children will grow, not only in wisdom and stature, but also in favor with God and man (Luke 2:52).

11

A Word to Children

Children have difficulty understanding why they must obey their parents. Scripture is specific on this responsibility: "Children, obey your parents in the Lord: for this is right" (Ephesians 6:1). In Ephesians Paul outlines the eternal plan of God, which is to unite all things (1:1-13). Such unity was made possible through the sacrifice of Jesus. Because of Him, oneness can be achieved among people, despite their differences (2:11-22). Within the church that unity is to be demonstrated (3:10). Paul enjoins all Christians to live in that unity (4:1-16). He further outlines some of the attitudes that will maintain unity (4:25—5:22).

Since it is God's purpose to unite all, it is the devil's purpose to work toward disunity. He is looking for any opportunity to cut into unity (4:27). When he succeeds, the Spirit of God is grieved (4:30). If we do not manifest the characteristics that can foster unity, and if we do not put away bitterness, wrath, clamor, and slander (4:31), we oppose God's plan (1:10). We give opportunity to the devil (4:27), and we grieve the Holy Spirit (4:30).

Immediately after developing God's plan for initiating and maintaining unity, Paul begins to outline the responsibilities of people in the home (5:21—6:4). Why? The answer is clear: if husbands are not loving their wives, if wives are not submitting to their husbands, if children are not obeying parents, and if parents are provoking children to wrath, there will be disunity in the home. *It is impossible to have unity in the church if there is disunity in the homes.*

Children who do not obey their parents introduce disunity into the home and the church. They act in opposition to God's plan, give opportunity to the devil, and grieve the Holy Spirit. That is serious! To fail to obey parents is to rebel against God's will and to prevent the potential blessings of Christ's death (unity of mankind).

Failing to obey parents is also rebelling against one's own well-being. That is why Paul adds, "that it may be well with you, and that you may live long upon the earth" (6:3). What does obedience to parents have to do with personal well-being? Alienation in family relationships affects the total person. It affects both physical and psychological health. A person is not at ease with himself when living amidst alienation. It affects sociological health. A person who cannot obey his parents has a difficult time relating well to any authority in society. Thus school and career days are affected. Even a person's role in marriage will be affected, for the capacity to submit to a marital mate is lessened when he has not been able to submit to his parents. Selfishness becomes a life-style. Alienation affects spiritual health—our relationship to God cannot be divorced from our relationship to parents, for it is His will that children obey them. Relationship to Christ cannot be complete, for His example was to be subject to Mary and Joseph (Luke 2:51).

Unwillingness to obey parents brings insecurity to both the children and the parents. Parents need the loving response of their children. A child's relationship with his parents helps meet some of his basic needs. The father has a need to express authority; he needs the child's respect for him as leader of the family. In loving him, the child should give him cooperation and the luxury of making mistakes. After all, doesn't he make allowances for your mistakes? If a child does not respect his father and obey him, the father's leadership growth will lessen and may become insecure in his headship role.

The mother has a basic need to express tenderness,

care, and peacemaking. If a child does not allow his mother this expression, her femininity will lessen and her insecurity will mount. Since a woman tends to take things personally, a child cannot rebel without deeply hurting his mother. She needs the words "I love you," from her children. She also has a part in "having dominion," for both male and female were given the ability to have dominion (Genesis 1:28). The mother best expresses her dominion over the things of household management (Proverbs 31:10 ff.), but if her desire to express love to her children is blocked, she may fill that vacuum by trying to dominate both her children and husband. Thus, a child's failure to obey may be a major factor in the blurring of roles, and this causes a serious identity crisis among youth.

Without seeing at home how the male is meant to function and how the female is meant to function, young people can become confused about their own roles. On the one hand, they may not like what they see in their sex role as observed in the mother or father. They may then decide to adopt the characteristics of the other sex. On the other hand, not liking what they see in the other sex role as observed at home, they may decide to have intimate relations with only their own sex, thus creating homosexuality. No wonder Paul wrote, "Obey your parents, for this is right."

Young people, don't bring insecurity to your parents. When you are out later than usual without phoning your parents, they will spend a sleepless night. Why? Because they love you. Is that a crime? You need to consider the kind of society in which we are living. Every day girls are abused, raped, and murdered. Every day boys are killed or permanently injured by auto accidents. Your parents have no way of knowing you are safe when you are out beyond your curfew, unless you call them. Be fair. Take away their anxiety; show them the consideration and love that you expect from them. Call them! Now, how do you get along with your brothers and sisters? Be a friend to them by setting a good example for them. If you think that familiarity breeds contempt, that you cannot be close friends with your siblings because you live with them and know them too well, what makes you think you can be part of a happy marriage later? You will be living with that mate and will know him or her well. Try to treat your brothers and sisters at least as well as you treat company.

Try to bring into your home life the characteristics of God as outlined in 1 Corinthians 13. As a son or daughter, as a brother or sister, be kind and patient. Don't be arrogant, or demand your own way. Rejoice in the good of your family members. This kind of life is not for adults only, but for Christians always.

As a young person, you are not just the church of tomorrow. You are also part of the church of today. You can help the family of God have the life-style needed in the church as you live your life according to God's will and God's role for you in the home. God knows better than you do the way you should go. He knows your development demands the authority of your parents. If this were not His intention, He would have given us other instructions. Evidently we all need the instructions He gave. If this is not followed, your healthy adjustment will be greatly hampered.

I can just hear you saying, "But my folks don't understand me!" This is doubtful, but if that is so, how about you? Do you "do unto others as you want them to do unto you"? Do you try to understand your parents? Do you listen? Do you pray for them by name? Do you live to help meet their needs, or do you want all of life to be centered around your needs, wants, and desires? Do not demand to be the center of attention. A secure family rests largely upon the fact that the mother and father can cleave to each other. If you give your mother the freedom to allow your father to be her center of attention, and give your father the freedom to allow your mother to be his center of attention, your needs will be met. Never act in such a way as to pit them against each other. Too many children play that game, little realizing that by weakening the cleaving relationship between the mother and father they are lessening the security of the home, and with it their own security.

If you will help your parents cleave to one another, you will make a major contribution to your home life. Obey your parents, therefore, and put on compassion, kindness, humility, gentleness, and endurance. Put up with one another. If you have a complaint against a family member, forgive. Above all, put on love, for love can bind the family into a really harmonious unit (Colossians 3:12-14).

12

Sex in Marriage

God designed the differences between the two sexes, and what God was not ashamed to create, we should not be ashamed to consider. If anyone should be free to discuss what God designed, Christians should. People have tried to keep the topic of sex hushed in order to keep our society "pure." I will admit that we have done a good job of keeping the subject out of the church, but I am not ready to admit that doing so has helped our society. Just look around. Aren't we living in a sex-perverted society? For years we have been needing to teach God's perspective of sex. Failure to do so has contributed by default to the free-love idea that now fills literature and the media.

What is sex? It is more than just the physical characteristics of the male and female. Sex refers to all that relates to being a male or female, including the psychological and emotional as well as the physical. In former chapters some of the basic differences between male and female were discussed. Let us now consider the teaching of God about the physical expression between the marriage partners and about sex education in the home.

What are the functions of sexual expression between a wife and husband? Of course, one function is for childbearing (Genesis 1:28). This is not the only function, however. Through sexual intimacy each mate meets a need of the other (2:18). If this were not a part of what is meant by "a helper suitable for him," God would not have built the female (2:18, 22; NASB). Neither would Paul have written, "Let the husband fulfill his duty to his wife, and likewise also the wife to her husband" (1 Corinthians 7:3; NASB).

Paul was referring to sexual intimacy (vv. 2-7). Another function is companionship (Genesis 2:18, 24). Still another is to prevent sin (1 Corinthians 7:5).

This is to emphasize that sexual intimacy between husband wife is a normal part of living, that it is to be a regular part of their life together. It is not something to be endured, but to be enjoyed. From Sarah in the Old Testament we find a beautiful expression about sex. She was ninety years old when she received the promise that she would become pregnant. Knowing the sexual intimacy necessary to become pregnant, Sarah said, "After I am waxed old shall I have pleasure?" (Genesis 18:12). She was questioning whether she would really experience that pleasure of youth again.

Adjustment to each other takes time. Even in ancient times a newly married man was allowed to be free from business and military service for a whole year, so that he and his wife could adjust to each other in every level of life (Deuteronomy 24:5). Growing together as mates is a lifetime process, and growing in the ways of sexual intimacy is one aspect of that process. Therefore, for a husband or wife to refuse to engage in sexual intimacy, except by mutual consent for an agreed period of time, is to fail to love one another and jeopardize the other's morality (1 Corinthians 7:3-5). At the same time, there are times when one mate knows that intimacy would not be enjoyable to the other. An understanding, loving mate would not put the other in the position of having to refuse. Being understanding would in itself be a gesture of love; however, one partner should not make a habit of communicating lack of sexual response. The body of each mate belongs to the other. Each should be exposed openly to the other without shame, and allow the other to explore (not exploit).

Neither mate should ever use sex as a means to get his way. Their bodies belong to each other. If one keeps it from the other, that one is stealing from the other. If a woman uses sex to induce her mate to buy her a new coat, or make a decision in her favor, she is no better than a prostitute. Sex then is lowered to the *eros* (selfish) level, and is no more on the *agape* (self-giving) level. All sexual expressions should be filled with *agape*-love, each person meeting the needs of the other. This calls for understanding what excites and pleases the other. It calls for patience and care.

Although sexual expression as an expression of love is normal and right within marriage, some guidelines are necessary. This is mentioned because of some false teaching concerning the application of Hebrews 13:4, which reads: "Let marriage be held in honor among all, and let the marriage bed be undefiled; for fornicators and adulterers God will judge" (Hebrews 13:4; NASB). This verse teaches that neither marriage nor the marriage bed is to be downgraded. Before the first century ended, some leaders were teaching that Christians should neither marry (1 Timothy 4:3) nor have intimacy if they were married. The writer of Hebrews denies both positions.

The misapplication of this verse stems from the problem of the text itself. The words "let" and "among all" are not in the original manuscript. This makes for two possible readings, the one quoted above and this one: "Marriage is honorable in everything—" Those who support this reading apply the words "in everything" to all varieties of sexual expression between husband and wife. They say that no matter what happens between the husband wife in the bed, the bed is undefiled. This is basically true; however, some use this interpretation to force their mates into all kinds of unpleasantries without mutual consent or mutual fulfillment. Some psychologists use this text and advocate sexual perversions to which the wife especially must submit.

The immediate context, "Let marriage be held in honor and let the marriage be undefiled" makes better reading, because of the word "for" that follows: "*For* God will condemn the immoral and adulterous." The marriage bed certainly is not undefiled in everything, because immorality and adultery are immediately excluded.

The word for "marriage bed" is *koite*, from which our English word "coitus" comes. Coitus refers to the natural conveying of semen to the female reproductive tract. (See Leviticus 15:16 ff.) Hebrews 13:4 is saying, "Let the natural sexual expression, which is intercourse, be undefiled." When would it be defiled? By adultery or sexual perversion.

When would there be sexual perversion between the husband and wife? Rather than list any specific acts, I would suggest that perversion is any act that degrades the beauty, the unity, and the love of the intimacy. I suggest the following criteria to determine when this happens: (1) when the act of sex is for selfish gratification only, without concern for the other's need; (2) when it is not an act of unity; that is, when both do not voluntarily give themselves to the other; (3) when one mate exploits the other.

No mate has the right to force the other. We are to love persons, not practices. We must control the passions, not let passions control us. Sexual intimacies between husband and wife need not be restricted to just one kind (intercourse), but both mates should mutually share in the expressions of any intimacy in *agape*-love. There are three possible levels of sexual expression within marriage: the instinct level (selfish pleasure), the duty level, and the *agape* level (seeing a need and moving to meet it).

On the *agape* level, each mate learns how the other is fulfilled and has the patience needed to fulfill the other's needs. Husbands and wives must discuss openly how each is stimulated in sexual intimacy. Real love-making is giving, not just receiving.

I am convinced that few sex problems exist between

husbands and wives, but there are many *self* problems. Sexual problems do not begin by how two people get into bed, but how they get *out* of bed, and their interpersonal relationship during the day. Compatibility and fidelity in sex begin with the Holy Spirit who frees people to live for others.

One of the misunderstandings about physical expressions is that they should be restricted to the bedroom. Meaningful physical expressions can include such things as rubbing the mate's back, holding hands, caressing, walking together, eating by candlelight, and expressing the beauties of the other. Read The Song of Solomon and ask yourself, "How long has it been since I spoke like that to my wife?" Another question that relates directly to the wife's sexual response is, "How long has it been since I have spoken in kindness and listened with interest to my wife?" The woman is sexually stimulated by the intimacy of conversation, not necessarily conversation about sex, but about the things that interest her. In this her selfhood can become exposed and invested in the life of her listener. Sharing the inner self with the other during the day is necessary for a satisfying sharing of the body during the night. Many wives feel certain that "he loves my body, but not *me*." Minds, attitudes, and feelings must be exposed to each other, not just bodies, in order for the basic needs of personhood to be met.

To find the way to the most satisfying sex life with each other, spend more time talking with each other and being interested in each other's thoughts and activities. Many married people have become sexually involved with a person outside of their marriage, not because of the attraction of their bodies, but because they listened to each other. That kind of concern is sexually attractive because sex involves the whole person, not just the body. That sex is merely a bodily function is a grave error being communicated by the mass media today.

When should we begin to teach our children about sex? The day they are born. Sex refers to how persons, not just physiques, function. Our children learn their earliest lessons about sex by observing the male and female roles of the parents at home.

When children become inquisitive about the physical side of sex, we need to answer them honestly. How we answer them will mold their attitudes about sex. If we act shocked at their questions, we communicate to them that sex is dirty. If we give a complicated lecture, we communicate that sex is complex and boring. If we answer them clearly, but honestly, we communicate that sex is another natural part of God's design for life. We must also question our children to find out exactly what they want to know. A brief answer to a specific question is usually sufficient for young children.

As the children reach adolescence, we should teach them about the stewardship of the body. God made it possible for people to become parents early in life. We should therefore teach our children that God considers us to be trustworthy with our bodies. We especially need to teach girls that boys are stimulated by sight and touch, that petting leads them to an emotional pitch that cannot always be intellectually stopped. Girls must understand that when a boy says he tingles all over when he touches her he is simply expressing a normal reaction. Our children need guidance and truth. They need our help most when they want it the least!

The best sex education children can receive is to see the mother and father live within their God-given roles of male and female, and to see how they love one another. The parents' leaving, cleaving, and oneness will provide the children with the best security possible. When children live within that security and realize that they are loved, respected, and trusted, many of the fears about their sexual explorations before marriage will diminish.

13

The Problem Clinic

Marriage is not all problems, but problems will arise even in the best of marriages. Most of the problems between married partners can be resolved happily by Christlike persons who have proper interpersonal communication.

Marriage does not necessarily make a person different. Husbands often say, "My wife has made me grouchy." This is doubtful. Family living has a remarkable way of bringing out a person's real characteristics. The real person is revealed. When problems arise, it is important not to look for the faults in the mate, but to look for weak spots within oneself. Fill in the weak spots with the unselfish act of giving self for the other's good. Let your reactions spring from your inner self, not from the actions of another. If you react to a person in the same manner he acts toward you, you are not being controlled by the indwelling Christ.

James speaks directly on this point. He wrote that each Christian will encounter all kinds of trials that will test his character (James 1:2). These trials are for the purpose of testing his faith. When the trials come, he should display endurance in having God's kind of reaction to them (1:3, 4). To do this, we each need wisdom, which James tells us God is willing to provide (v. 5). This does not refer to intellectualism, but to the characteristics James describes (3:13 ff.): "Who is a wise man and endued with knowledge among you? let him shew out a good conversation [good conduct] his works with meekness of wisdom." This wisdom from God is "first pure [without ulterior motives], then peaceable, gentle, and easy to be intreated [open to reason], full of mercy and good fruits, without partiality, and without hypocrisy [insincerity]" (v. 17).

The situation should not determine our lives, but rather the characteristics we pour into those situations. The solution to many marital problems can be discovered if two people will list the situation in a middle column, then list Christlike characteristics on one side and opposite characteristics on the other. Then each mate should examine himself as to which of the two opposing attitudes he is pouring into the threatening situation. Some of these attitudes and their opposites are: peaceable—striving; gentle—harsh; reasonable—stubborn; kind—unkind; self-controlled—tempermental; jealous—not jealous; humble—arrogant; forgiving—resentful; thoughtful—inconsiderate; gracious—ungracious; honest—dishonest.

While one mate may be wrong in his action, the other should not be wrong in reacting. Consistent expression of Christ's way by just one person can revolutionize the relationship of a family.

Let us consider some specific problems and possible solutions.

1. *Who should manage the finances?* The one who is more responsible and capable in keeping records straight. If the wife handles the money, she must remember that this is a delegated responsibility, and must manage the budget in keeping with the life goals of the household.

2. *Should both the husband and wife work?* This is becoming a common practice. Families have varying situations, so it is impossible to make a general rule for all persons to follow. Both persons, however, should ask themselves why they are both working. Is it to meet the necessities of the family, or just to keep up with the crowd? Once the wife's salary is budgeted to help with the monthly bills, there is no easy exit in sight. If her salary could be used for extras, she could later discontinue working without undue hardship.

3. *My husband wants sex too much. What can I do about it?* Read 1 Corinthians 7:1-7. The man has been planning on sex with you even before the wedding. He fully expects sex after the wedding, even though you may not have had the indication that he was so "sex-minded." Your relationship has changed now that you are married, and you have a responsibility in that change. Be thankful that he loves you. He could have his sex needs met elsewhere, if you do not seek to fulfill them.

4. *We do not want to have children. Is this wrong?* Many young couples feel this way. Others must not cause them to feel unacceptable if they are childless. Sexual expression is not just for creation of life, but also for the cementing of love. Although in the Bible children are considered to be a blessing (Psalm 127:4, 4), there is no "thus saith the Lord" that a couple should have children to be happy. Neither does the Bible inform us as to when a couple should have children or how many. Furthermore, birth control is not Biblically wrong; however, living just for oneself *is* wrong. Each couple should examine their motives.

5. *My husband does not show me physical affection except in bed. What can I do?* How do you look when he comes home from work? Look nice, smell nice, smile, and grab him! Show him physical affection, and it will be returned.

6. *My wife is fat and sloppy and unattractive. Why?* Is she working all day without modern conveniences? Do you give her a reason to look nice by taking her out to eat or to a movie? Do you buy her pretty clothes and compliment her when she does look nice? Compliment her on her looks, especially in public. Sweet talk her as when you were courting!

7. *Who is responsible for the children's discipline when the father is gone?* Specifically, the mother is; however, the matter of child discipline should have been discussed and agreed upon before the situation

107

arises. If this is done, one parent will uphold the other when both are involved, and when one parent is absent, the other will administer discipline in agreement with the other. To delay discipline until the father comes home is not effective discipline; furthermore, the children will dread to see Dad come home.

8. *What should be done if in-laws continually interfere?* The couple can permit the in-laws to volunteer advice. Listening to them may meet a need of theirs. Listen without comment and then do what the two of you have agreed upon. Never allow the in-laws to polarize you. If they become insistent or overbearing, be honest enough to tell them how you feel. Explain that you are a new family unit over which the husband is the head.

9. *What should parents do when their unwed daughter gets pregnant, or their son is the one involved?* Do not add a wrong reaction to a wrong action. Do not force the two to marry, if a lifelong commitment is obviously not desired. Do not act just to "save face." The only difference between this sin and the sins you commit is that theirs becomes obvious. Whether or not the daughter should keep the child will depend upon the unified decision of the family, after considering the welfare of both the child and the mother.

10. *What would you advise for a family in which the husband and wife are of different faiths?* This need not be the tragedy that some people make it. Of course, nagging or belittling the other's position is never wise. God wants the man and wife to live in peace. Providing that both have centered their "faith" in Jesus Christ, the following approach may help:

List the areas of agreement between the two religions. You may be surprised to find that you agree far more than you disagree. Thank God together for the specific points of agreement. Read and discuss the Bible together systematically and regularly. Study openly together the areas of disagreement, but do not allow the study to blur the points of agreement. Let the points of disagreement be seen in the Scriptural context, with the aim to understand truth and not to support a personal position. Decide together to let the Bible be the authority. The study should consider all the Bible says about a certain question. Do not argue about your differences. Ask, "Is this difference essential to Christianity?" Practice the patience and loving-kindness of God.

11. *What if the husband has interests and activities that are uninteresting to the wife, or vice versa?* The one should try to learn about the other's interest—read about it, ask questions, join in it, and try to develop an interest. If that is not possible, try these things: allow the other to pursue the activity without complaining or sarcasm. Develop your own interest or hobby that you can pursue when the other is occupied. In other words, respect his desires and keep busy yourself. Plan and encourage activities that you both enjoy, and spend some time together. Make the time so pleasant that the mate will want to have more of these "together" times than "apart" times.

12. *How can we foster family togetherness?* Do things together around the house. Make it a family project to wash the car, plant shrubbery, paint the house, rearrange the furniture. Have home parties with popcorn, cokes, and sandwiches, or have an indoor picnic on the floor. Let the whole family contribute in making a pizza, adding the ingredients each likes best. Sing together, play together, sit around a campfire in your own backyard, sit on the patio and listen to the sounds of nature. Play outdoor games. Turn off the TV and communicate with each other. Play board games that involve the whole family. Ask the children for their opinions and advice about family plans and purchases. Let the whole family take part in buying a house or car. Take the children with

you when you buy a present for your mate. Include the children in conversations about work, finances, or decisions. This will help them to understand and accept the fact that they cannot have everything they want. Plan your vacations together, the schedule, route, activities, places to stay. Read the Bible together. Choose a passage that applies to a specific need or problem In the family. Allow each family member to raise questions. Discuss together the implications of the Scripture. Pray together for specific needs by naming friends of all the members.

13. *How can I keep my wife feeling that she is a person with dignity?* Recognize her charisma (gift) and encourage her to use it. Praise her abilities in front of others. Pass on to her the compliments you hear about her. Trust her. Don't make jokes about her to others. Do not criticize, belittle, or oppose her in front of the children. Protect her against their rebellion. Do not allow them to show disrespect for her or disobedience. Support her disciplinary measures. Help her once in a while with the housework. Stay at home with the children occasionally so she can go out by herself or with a friend. Take her with you to as many public gatherings as you can. Tell her you love her. Share with her your dreams and desires. Take time to satisfy her in the sex act.

14. *What should be done when a husband spends much of his time at the office or traveling in his work?* If the husband's absence from home is because his job necessitates it and he is happy in that work, it is up to the wife to accept the unalterable circumstances and adjust to it. It is much better to have a husband who is happy and contented, even though absent, than to have a husband who is restless and unhappy, even though at home. If the wife is lonely and bored while he is away, she can become involved in service for others, hobbies, and keep contact with friends and neighbors. When her husband comes home, she

should devote herself fully to him, keeping the household tasks to a minimum, preparing his favorite foods, and listening to his adventures. Make his time at home a time of great quality, since it cannot be of great quantity. Husband, when you come home from a trip, devote time to the family. Don't plunge immediately into your business at home. Also, if you have been away very long, your wife has been making all the decisions. She will need time to adjust to the fact that the head of the family is back.

If the absence is voluntary and not necessary, the wife should then examine herself and the home atmosphere. Is she bitter, angry, and upset whenever he is home? Are all of her duties and services burdensome? Is the house cluttered and he is a person who likes everything in its place? Is it such a showplace that he is not free to remove his shoes while he reads the newspaper? Perhaps the wife is not in agreement with his type of work and pleads with him to change. Maybe she is so independent and self-sufficient that she does not seem to need his presence at all. If any of these hit the target, the two need to work at being one in their life goals.

The Church's Responsibility to Families

This entire book has called for an emphasis on family togetherness. Our complex multischeduled lives would prevent the family from being together, unless we get our priorities in place. Let us not be an activity-controlled people. The church should not be a factor in keeping family members apart all week. Here are some suggestions for churches:

1. Develop the philosophy that the church exists for families, not vice versa. Evaluate every lesson, every sermon, and every activity according to how it will affect the family life of the members.

2. Plan activities that the family can attend together. Why have the youth program just for youth?

What about having family programs? Why not rent the roller rink for the whole family once in a while? Let two or three families plan and present the Sunday evening worship program once a month.

3. Recognize family units more. The whole family could come forward when a member makes a decision for Christ. Have family members baptize each other.

4. Use family units to serve Communion and take up the offering during the worship service. What Scripture restricts these tasks to elders and deacons? *None!*

5. For one quarter of the year the Sunday school could have a class for families. Why split up the families every Sunday for years and years?

6. Establish a Christian counseling center in the area. The area churches could hire a Christian counselor who would be available for family counseling.

7. Let your preacher be a family man. Do not expect him to attend every meeting of the church. He needs some time at home with his family.

8. Seek to utilize the members of the church in combination with their family members, not in isolation from them.

9. Publish in the church paper each week information about a family, sharing their names, addresses, and activities in school and community, careers, and church work.

10. Finish all the committee meetings in one or two nights a week instead of separating family members every night of the week.

The church must declare war upon the present trend to keep the family separated. Heaven will be God's family living together in unity; may a foretaste of that reality be present here on earth. May each of us allow Heaven on earth as we let the image of God shine out of our hearts at home. If we have received the Holy Spirit, let us walk with Him and create the community of unity and maintain it.